FREE AT LAST

A Cup of Water, a Death Sentence,
and an Inspiring Story of
One Woman's Unwavering Faith

ASIA BIBI
WITH
Anne-Isabelle Tollet

BroadStreet
PUBLISHING

BroadStreet Publishing® Group, LLC
Savage, Minnesota, USA
www.broadstreetpublishing.com

FREE AT LAST: A Cup of Water, a Death Sentence,
and an Inspiring Story of One Woman's Unwavering Faith

Enfin Libre! © 2020, Groupe Elidia
Éditions du Rocher
28, rue Comte Félix Gastaldi
BP 521—98015 Monaco
www.editionsdurocher.fr

978-1-4245-6072-1 (paperback)
978-1-4245-6073-8 (e-book)

Stock or custom editions of BroadStreet Publishing titles may be purchased in bulk for educational, business, ministry, fundraising, or sales promotional use. For information, please email info@broadstreetpublishing.com.

Cover and interior by Garborg Design at GarborgDesign.com

Printed in the United States of America

20 21 22 23 24 5 4 3 2 1

For Eisha and Eisham

CONTENTS

INTRODUCTION

It is not because things are difficult that we do not dare;
it is because we do not dare that they are difficult.
SENECA

It felt like floating between a dream and reality when, on Wednesday, October 31, 2018, at 5:47 a.m., I received a brief phone call from Ashiq.

"Good morning," he said. "Asia Bibi is free. Congratulations!"

The long-awaited day had finally arrived: the Supreme Court of Pakistan acquitted Asia Bibi. What incredible joy! But it would be short-lived. After three days of quasi-civil war provoked by the Islamists, the Pakistani government made a U-turn and signed an agreement with the Islamists on November 3. The agreement prevented Asia from leaving the country before the court processed an application for judicial review of the acquittal. Despite my experience of Pakistan as one of the most unpredictable countries I know, I still felt deeply distraught, and so did Asia's family.

Such disillusion! Cut to the quick, I was back at square one but undaunted. After eight long years of tireless efforts, now was not the time to throw in the towel. In the struggle against religious extremism, everything played out in the final round. I put all of my strength, courage, and determination into ending the fight with a knockout.

Thanks to unprecedented media mobilization in both the national and international press, and with the help of the highest political authorities, Asia Bibi was smuggled out of her prison cell in the middle of the night on November 7 before heading abroad six months later with her family, who was also receiving death threats.

I was finally going to hear Mrs. Asia Bibi with my own ears and see her with my own eyes. I had hoped for so long to meet her! After her first death sentencing in November 2010, I submitted myriad requests to the Pakistani authorities for permission to visit her in prison but to no avail. A Western woman, and a journalist to boot, should not relay this dark story, which brings Pakistan no honor, to the global press.

When I moved to Pakistan in 2008 as a permanent correspondent for a twenty-four-hour news channel, I never imagined that I would find myself leading this unlikely struggle with its many unforeseen developments. How many times had I shown up outside her prison in Sheikhupura with a bag of oranges in hand, passing myself off as a humanitarian worker or dressed as a Pakistani woman, to coax the sometimes unscrupulous guards into letting me in? It never worked. Even though I, too, received threats from Islamists, it was important to me to break the *omertà* so that her story would be heard around the world.

It all started one morning in November 2010. I was reading the English translation of the Pakistani press when I stumbled across a brief article stating that Asia Bibi, a young Christian woman, had just been condemned to death for blasphemy. According to the article, she had insulted the Prophet Muhammad. Pope Benedict XVI asked the Pakistani courts to review the judgment and grant her clemency. Immediately, the country ignited, and the most influential, radical religious parties set up demonstrations across the country to denounce the Catholic Church for meddling in the affairs of the Islamic Republic of Pakistan. I followed those demonstrations during which hateful extremists demanded death by hanging for Asia Bibi.

I became close to Asia Bibi's family and promised to never abandon them, even when I returned to France. To this today, that bond remains unbroken. I've since written two books, *Blasphemy*[1] and *Death Is Not a Solution*,[2] to continue the fight against religious obscurantism, a nondivisive issue that is neither political nor religious. I have received worldwide support not only from millions of Christians but also from the Muslim and Jewish communities. The issue of blasphemy is a highly sensitive one, so I took the liberty of addressing the matter with Pope

---

1 *Blasphème*, XO édition, May 2011.
2 *La Mort n'est pas une solution*, Éditions du Rocher, March 2015.

Francis directly and asked him not to intervene, as doing so might aggravate the situation in Pakistan. He listened.

This fight also led me to deliver speeches at the United Nations in both New York and Geneva. The European Parliament voted on a resolution in support of Asia Bibi. The mayors of Paris, Madrid, Bordeaux, Le Mans, La Flèche, and La Brède all responded to my call to make Asia Bibi the citizen of honor in their towns and cities. French presidents Nicolas Sarkozy, François Hollande, and Emmanuel Macron spoke to their Pakistani counterparts, encouraging them to defend the values of justice and respect human rights in a society that is increasingly subject to religious fanaticism.

Through the Asia Bibi International Committee,[3] an organization I founded in 2015, I collected numerous testimonials of support from around the world. Thanks to her husband, Ashiq, these were relayed to Asia in her tiny cell. In return, she let me know that these gestures of sympathy gave her a sense of hope—the hope of recovering her freedom.

Asia Bibi became, very much in spite of herself, a symbol of the way the blasphemy law has gone adrift and of how it is so often abused to settle personal conflicts by spreading false accusations. In 1860, British colonial authority put into place the blasphemy law, which spares neither Muslims nor religious minorities. General Muhammad Zia-ul-Haq made the law even

---

3   www.asiabibi.com

more severe in 1986 under his dictatorship as part of his initiative to Islamize society.

The assassinations of the governor of the Punjab and then the Federal Minister for Minorities affairs in 2011 stifled any attempts at productive debate and reform within the government, and tensions around the issue grew. In this regard, Pakistani Prime Minister Imran Khan made a great show of bravery by publicly acknowledging the Supreme Court's decision to acquit Asia Bibi.

Once she was finally free and in a free country, I thought it would be easy to find the woman for whom I had been the spokesperson for all these years. But because of continued death threats from Islamists, Asia Bibi is no longer safe anywhere, and I had a difficult time locating her in Canada. When I found myself standing in front of the door to her house, a bouquet of white roses in hand, my heart raced. I rang the doorbell, but it was not working. I knocked feebly three times and received no response. I heard pots clanging in the kitchen over the voice of a woman speaking Urdu.

It's her, yes, it's her! I said to myself. I was worried, intimidated, and scared of frightening this family who wasn't expecting visitors, because nobody—myself included—was supposed to know their address. I knocked on the door again, this time a little louder, and then waited a few seconds before calling Ashiq's name. I knew he would recognize me immediately because I had seen him several times in Pakistan as well as in France, Spain, and Switzerland.

The door finally opened, and Ashiq, whom I had always known to wear traditional Pakistani garb, appeared in front of me decked out in a trendy tracksuit. Clinging to my bouquet of flowers as one would a flotation device, I felt flustered. Ashiq didn't seem to recognize me, and without a word or a smile, he gestured for me to enter. Once inside, he gave me a big hug. Over his shoulder, I spotted a small woman with a round face and long black hair tied up in a ponytail. Asia looked at me, dumbstruck. I struggled to grasp that she was truly there, in the flesh, and I was standing before her. I had pictured meeting her for the first time on an airport runway, like the way people meet when a hostage is returned.

Ashiq muttered a few words in Urdu, and Asia's face lit up before enveloping me in her gentleness. I couldn't get over it; the woman whose suffering I had reported on for years was finally by my side. She hugged me hard, the way my daughter does, and pressed her head to my chest. Asia seemed to regard me as a member of her family who might disappear at any moment. I was relieved and deeply moved.

"Thank you. Thank you for everything you did for me. If I am alive and free, it is thanks to you and the support of God. You saved my life. You are an angel, my soul sister," she said.

I heard her voice for the first time. A voice that did not tremble despite all her trials and suffering, but a voice that was powerful, alive, and sparkling. I wanted to take her face between my hands, but that seemed too intimate and premature. I put both of my hands on her shoulders, smiled affectionately, and responded, "I have been waiting for you, Asia."

Then her two daughters, Eisha and Eisham, who had been watching the scene unfold, took me in their arms as their parents, now emotional, stood by. Asia then invited me to sit down and offered me Pakistani tea. On the couch in their suburban house, we spent a long time recounting the last ten years, so happy and relieved to have them behind us. I asked Asia if she was in good health, and she responded with a candid yes, even though she sometimes had a few head pains. I was struck by how strong, smart, and brave this small woman was.

Asia Bibi's acquittal established a precedent in Pakistan. Now, anyone who makes false accusations of blasphemy will, in turn, face harsh consequences. Her freedom was certainly a complete, collective victory. A chain of support forged around the world, and it raised awareness among the media, politicians, and nongovernmental organizations (NGOs).

Without the commitments of so many individuals, the mother of two would have never again seen her children, who were deprived of her for ten years. Asia Bibi is able to hold her daughters in her arms and cover them in kisses once again, and that is thanks to countless people who supported her and prayed for her from all corners of the globe. And for that, I will never be able to say thank you enough!

Anne-Isabelle Tollet

Chapter 1

IN THE DARK

The future is also about memory.
DENYS GAGNON

I'm not the type to remember dates, but some days you never forget. Like Wednesday, June 9, 2010. Before sunset, I had arrived at Sheikhupura detention center, where I was to spend three years before changing prisons the way one moves to a new house. I hadn't been tried yet, but I was already guilty in everyone's eyes. I remember that day as though it were yesterday, and when I close my eyes, I relive every moment of it.

My wrists were on fire, and I struggled to breathe. My neck, which my youngest child loved to wrap her arms around, was squeezed into an iron collar that the guard could tighten at will with a huge locknut. A long chain dragged across the filthy floor, connecting my throat to the wrist of the guard, who pulled me along like a dog on a leash. Deep down inside of me, a gnawing fear pulled me into the depths of darkness. A nagging fear that would never leave me. At precisely that moment, I wanted to escape the harshness of this world.

Leather cuffs strapped my ankles, and a taut, narrow chain connected them. I nearly fell with each step. Between standing and stooping, I struggled to move forward. I shuffled in my sandals, which were made by the kind cobbler in my village. My loose hair bothered me. I had lost my headscarf when the police threw me like a sack of potatoes out of the police vehicle that brought me to the prison. I felt naked and bare without my scarf. My untied hair hid part of my grimy, sweaty face. I must have looked like a lady of the night. I grimaced in pain. The guard failed to notice because he refused to turn around and look at me out of fear of "dirtying" himself. Suddenly, his pace quickened, and he pulled abruptly on the chain tied to my neck. I fell flat on my face onto the ground, but he didn't slow down. The collar started to suffocate me, so I quickly scrambled back onto my feet and in step behind him.

In the distance, I heard dishes clanging against one another. I looked down the endless corridor one way and then the other, but all I saw were closed wooden doors. I jumped at a woman's sudden cry: "Death!"

Other women took up a chant: "Hang her! Hang her! Hang her!"

I realized the prisoners, who were penned in here like livestock, were shouting their hatred for me. Full of fear, and to escape those dark cries, I hummed to myself through a clenched jaw to drown out their words, but the effort was in vain. I stared at a large fly resting on one of the filthy neon lights in the long, pallid hallway. In successive waves, the prisoners beat their dishes together in step: "The rope!" *Clack, clack...*"The rope!" *Clack, clack...*

The guard stopped short in front of the last cell in the corridor and turned around for the first time. His eyes bulged with satisfaction. From under his navy-blue beret, sweat streamed down his body. Big wet rings seeped out of his armpits. He pulled a dirty old rag out of his pocket.

I could hear new jeers: "Death to the blasphemer! Blasphemy, blasphemy! Put her to death!"

"Shut up," the guard shouted. "Shut up, you filthy bunch of females!"

Everyone went quiet. The silence made me want to throw up. The guard unscrewed my iron collar with the disgusting rag, careful not to come into direct contact with my hair or skin. I grimaced in pain, lowered my eyes, then lifted my hand to my bruise-covered neck.

With a look of revulsion on his face, he spit at me, "You're worse than a pig! I have to dirty myself by touching you and putting up with your rottenness, but hopefully that won't last for long. *Allah Akbar!*"

He kicked his boot into my kneecap, and I collapsed. I soon learned that this guard, with whom I would end up spending three years, was named Khalil. Khalil stooped over me to remove the cuffs that bound my feet. Cradling my knee with both hands, I held the pain inside and looked upon him fearfully.

While freeing my ankles, he cackled, "The death penalty! That's right. Death for insulting our Prophet! Who did you think you were?"

I said nothing.

While Khalil opened the creaking door to the cramped space that would become my home, I struggled to get up and then to stand on one foot to avoid putting pressure on my throbbing knee.

Laughing heartily, Khalil asked, "Did you hear your girl-friends? The next time I open this door, it will be to dangle you from a rope, *inshallah*!"

He pushed me, and I fell into the cell. He scraped his boots off on me as I lay there. The door slammed behind his sneering laugh. Sprawled out on the earthy ground of this hopeless cell, I stared at the door, thinking that perhaps God sent this hardship.

Chapter 2

I'LL TELL YOU EVERYTHING

The test of courage isn't dying but living.
VITTORIO ALFIERI, *ORESTE*

For a long time, I thought I was going to die because of a glass of water. It was a close call. I was condemned to hang and lost years of precious time because I was thirsty and drank out of the same cup as Muslim women on a day when temperatures reached over one hundred degrees. Because I, a Christian, served the water, my field companions judged it impure and accused me of blasphemy.

In Pakistan, blasphemy is the greatest crime of all. At the mere accusation of it, the *mullahs*, who lead mosques, refuse to leave you in peace. I didn't commit blasphemy; I was never blasphemous. But when faced with my village's *mullah*, who later filed an official complaint against me, I refused to renounce my faith in exchange for immediate liberation. I was subsequently imprisoned in 2009 and sentenced to hang in 2010.

Of course, the accusation against me was only a pretext to get rid of me. I have no proof, but I find the justification of my accusers rather dubious. My conviction condemned my entire family, who had always been happy in Pakistan. We are Christian, and even though we couldn't openly express our joy at being so, we respected Islam. Being a Christian in my country may not be advantageous, and fortunately, not all Christians are accused of blasphemy. Even Muslims aren't immune to such accusations. What I have come to understand is that all prejudices are fair game when it comes to getting rid of others and subjecting them to your personal will.

If only I'd known that one day a simple cup of fresh water would prevent me from watching my children grow up! I rotted in prison for more than nine years—nine years of torture and humiliation. For a long time, I asked myself why God was imposing so much suffering on me and my family. I wondered why religious extremists used me to spread terror in my country and why they were hammering away at my case so hard. In my little windowless cell, I fought against the darkness of my dungeon. And throughout all of those years, I lost my carefree nature and hope for a future. It was the fight of my life, and I was not prepared for it.

The legal saga gave way to an acquittal in October 2018 that was confirmed at the start of 2019. But in the face of the political and popular pressure for my death, I had to remain detained for another seven months for my own safety, while doubt hovered above my future. During the last few months of my detainment, rumors circulated that I had come to Canada. And finally, at the beginning of the month of May, I indeed arrived in Canada. What a whirlwind in ten years!

From the depths of my prison, I did not understand how much the international community supported me. How could I, a simple peasant at the age of fifty-four, imagine that I would become the global symbol of the fight against religious extremism. Yet my family and lawyer had told me as much: "Thanks to the French journalist, the world has taken an interest in the fate of the little uneducated peasant woman. Some very important people have committed to saving you."

That French journalist was Anne-Isabelle Tollet, who became my soul sister. For ten years, she moved heaven and earth, and thanks to her, my experience stirred the world. She gave me media exposure, which helped others support me, and I owe all of them my freedom today. It would take lifetimes for me to thank everyone who helped over the course of those years. I often wonder why they did so and what it is about me, among so many other suffering people, that could have interested them. God must have heard my prayers.

Two people in particular also played key roles in my exfiltration and have, until now, remained in the shadows. Without the help of Jan Figel, the European Union special correspondent for religious freedom, and Pakistani Muhammad Amanullah, my nickname for whom is Aman, I would still be under the watch of Pakistan's guards and far from my children. This ordeal also forced Aman to leave his country to avoid being murdered by the Islamists for apostasy. From Australia, he continues to defend people accused of blasphemy and, like me, is unable to return to his country.

Before leaving Pakistan in 2018, Aman's family was attacked by an angry mob, who seriously injured his sister and occupied his home. In 2014, my lawyer at the time had told me about a Pakistani Muslim who was simultaneously defending three Christian women accused of blasphemy. He had even passed himself off as the fiancé of one in order to obtain permission to visit her in jail. I called this man on the phone and asked if he could help me, and he did. He got in touch with lawyer Saif ul-Malook and convinced him to represent me before the Pakistan Supreme Court. Aman has never let me down, and even today, he acts as an interpreter when I want to talk to Anne-Isabelle. All three of us speak on the phone together, and we laugh a lot.

Now that I am free and living in a free country, I'm becoming increasingly aware that my story moved people and that rumors and false information about me have spread. This book is my chance to state a few truths. I wrote it with Anne-Isabelle, who is well-acquainted with my home country. She also helped me structure my thoughts and, of course, to write. It is not that I did not have the words; I simply did not know how to express them. I am illiterate and without formal education. I don't speak English or any language other than Urdu. However, I am learning English, thanks to Aman, who sends me little lessons all the way from Australia. I listen to them on my phone every day.

My name is Asia Noreen. I am the daughter of Salamat Masih, and I was born in January of 1965 in the Nankana Sahib district in the Punjab region. On my Pakistani ID, it says that I have a beauty mark on my right cheek, and I still have it. People know me as Asia Bibi, but *Bibi* is actually a nickname that literally translates to "grandmother" in Urdu. Over time, it became an honorific title given to ladies who are respectful, pure, and pious. In a strange twist of fate, both of my accusers are also named Bibi, as are many women in Pakistan. These days, I have changed my identity and pray that the religious extremists cannot find me. I am a political exile living under a fake name in a country where it is cold.

I am married to Ashiq, the father of my two children. Like many Pakistani Christians, Ashiq bears the name *Masih*, and I recently learned that it means "the Messiah" in Arabic. My life in Pakistan might seem complicated to those who live in the West. For example, in Pakistan, many parents arrange marriages for their children, and this tradition creates problems and confusion for many couples who are not allowed to marry for love. I had such an experience, yet through the grace of God, I have found peace and love with my beloved Ashiq and two daughters.

My case showed that politicians and the judiciary system are aware of the ways in which the blasphemy law is abused and misused. Sadly, despite my release, the climate does not seem to have changed, and Christians can expect all sorts of reprisals. In fact, shortly after I was freed, my cell became home to a new Christian woman sentenced to death for blasphemy. Shagufta Kausar, a mother of four children ages five to thirteen, and her husband, Shafqat Masih, were sentenced by a Pakistani court for having sent blasphemous text messages. The *imam*, a Muslim worship leader, of a local mosque had filed the complaint against them. According to his complaint, Shafqat Masih, with his wife's help, had sent text messages written in English that insulted the Prophet.

My lawyer, Saif ul-Malook, who returned to Pakistan after I was freed, is defending them. Despite threats, he wants to help the victims of the blasphemy law, which is exceptionally brave of him because he is a Muslim. With Saif as a lawyer, I think that Shagufta Kausar, the wife, will make it out alright. From what I know, both spouses are illiterate, so they couldn't have sent text messages in Urdu, let alone in English. It is yet another absurd accusation of blasphemy, and if the law did not destroy the lives of people, it would almost be laughable.

Although I am certain Pakistan will never repeal the blasphemy law, I would like for people to stop abusing it. Nobody should be treated as guilty without concrete proof. I pray every day for Shagufta Kausar and Shafqat Masih and everyone else accused of blasphemy, and I continue to solemnly ask Pakistan to reexamine the blasphemy law that nearly cost me my life.

I am blessed that my life resumed after I was freed. It was a true honor to see my children and my husband, my other half. I get to see their faces light up every day, and mine does too. I thank God that I am once again able to hold them close to my heart, which swells with love, innocence, and goodness. It is a miracle. I prayed relentlessly that I would be with them again, and it is thanks to their strength and unshakeable love that I was able to get through all of those years. They were the light in the darkness that allowed me to overcome my despair. We are now ready for a fresh start and perhaps a better life. But at what cost?

I am still haunted by prison. I am haunted by the silence that followed when I set down the metal cup of water that quenched my thirst. I am haunted by the cold and authoritarian silences that rhythmed my days between the cries of delirious crowds endlessly repeating, "Death to the Christian woman!" My heart broke when I had to leave without saying goodbye to my father and other members of my family. Pakistan is my homeland, but I am in exile forever. Before I was flown to Canada, the Pakistani authorities told me point-blank: "Your husband and children will be able to return to Pakistan in four years if they wish to, but you will never be allowed to return to your native land."

Perhaps you know my story from the media. Maybe you have imagined my ordeal and tried to put yourself in my shoes to understand my suffering. But you cannot picture my daily life, and that is why, in this book, I'll tell you everything.

Chapter 3

FIRST DEATH SENTENCE

You have to suffer to understand suffering.
ALBERTINE HALLE, *LA VALLÉE DES BLÉS D'OR*

I spent over a year rotting in a black hole of a prison cell before my first trial even took place. I was scared, but I had to put my trust in God rather than humanity. *God is stronger than death*, I would say to myself. On November 8, 2010, I showed up alone before the Nankana Sahib court. My family could not attend; it was too dangerous, and we didn't have the means to pay someone to defend me.

In that small, local courtroom, my accusers faced me: two women and the village *imam*. I also noticed three *mullahs* had made the journey, just for me. At the time, I didn't know their presence was to pressure the judge into convicting me lest he face their retaliation. I used to think that I had failed to proclaim my innocence, but now I understand that it did not matter what I said or did; I was already sentenced.

Memory sometimes fails me after nine years without seeing the stars, but a clear and precise memory of what I said to the judge on that day remains:

> I am a married woman. My husband is a manual laborer. I usually worked with a group of women in Muhammad Idree's fields, so I could earn a daily salary. On the day of business that I am being accused of, I was working there. Two of the women, Mafia Bibi and Asma Bibi, became angry with me because of the water I drank and then brought to them. They refused to touch it because I am a Christian. What followed was a heated discussion, and harsh words flew. Then they went to see Qari Salaam, the village *imam*, whose wife they knew. By conspiring with him, they made up a completely false accusation. When the police interrogated me, I swore on the Bible that I never said the slightest word against the Prophet Muhammad nor the Quran, both of which I have the utmost respect for. But the police were complicit in recording their false accusations.
>
> The two women wanted revenge. My ancestors have lived in this village since the founding of Pakistan, and as for me, in over forty years, I have never been the subject of any accusation of such kind. I have no education. There is no church in my vil-

lage. I do not know the religion of Islam. How could I make improper accusations against the Prophet and the Quran? My boss is not a neutral bystander either because he has family connections with the women who made the accusation against me.

That was how I proclaimed my truth. The judge with the long white beard scribbled on a little piece of graph paper and then asked the *mullah* of my village to provide his version of the facts. In my country, the word of a woman does not count, and even though the *mullah* had not been present to witness my alleged blasphemy, he lied:

> The accused Asia Bibi present in this here court-room declared in front of myself and others that the Prophet Hazrat Muhammad—may peace be with him—fell ill one month before his death and that as he was lying on his bed, insects came out of his mouth and ears. The accused furthermore declared that the Prophet Hazrat Muhammad—may peace be with him—married Hazrat Khadija Razi Anha out of financial interest and that after having entered into that marriage, he got rid of her. She added that the holy Quran is not a divine book since it was written and compiled by the Muslims.

At these words, I realized that the inhabitants in my village spread their hatred between smiles. No longer did I doubt that I was a victim of conspiracy and brutal malice. The judge thanked the *mullah* and announced that he would withdraw for a few minutes. He disappeared through a small door, and the policemen surrounding me told me to sit down. I understood the judge's need to think on the matter, and it gave me hope. Surely he couldn't believe for a second that I would say those horrible things. In my country, nobody can say such things without the risk of having acid thrown at you or being lynched by a crowd.

I lowered my head to avoid the hateful stares of the audience. I could feel their eyes piercing me, stabbing me, without yet knowing that those same eyes would haunt me every night for years to come. The judge returned after five minutes, and in the moment, his presence reassured me. I foolishly believed that the whole story was far too absurd for the judge to consider a single word of it. I inhaled a deep breath of courage before the announcement of the verdict, and then it broke out like a clap of thunder: "Asia Noreen Bibi, in accordance with Article 295 C of the Pakistani penal code, the court sentences you to capital punishment by hanging and a fine of three hundred thousand rupees."

His verdict still rings in my ears today. Time stopped. I could no longer move; I couldn't believe it. With a flick of his mallet, the judge had sentenced me to death. My mouth hung wide open as I gasped for air, as if I were drowning. Hot tears flooded my face, and nothing could stop the downpour. I didn't want to die. I buried my face into my knees to swallow my pain and to escape this act of hatred. I felt completely alone.

People who I didn't even know stood up to give the judge an impassioned ovation. They were celebrating my death, crying out, "Death to the Christian woman, *Allah Akbar*!" They hurled scathing and humiliating insults at me. The three *mullahs* smiled behind their tufted beards, applauding vigorously while exiting the courtroom. The cruelty in their joy overwhelmed me and sent a chill down my spine. How could the suffering of others make anyone feel so triumphant?

My face hot with anger and shame, I asked myself, *Why do these people hate me? Why had they lied? How could my life or death affect their existence? How can a person rejoice in the death of someone they do not know?* I was just a poor peasant. I had naively believed that they would recognize my innocence. I had done nothing wrong. I closed my eyes and prayed in my heart, *My God, Jesus, give me strength, I am not educated enough to understand ordinary madness.*

"Get a move on!" The policemen interrupted my thoughts and grabbed me roughly by the arms. They feared the crowd would become uncontrollable, so they me led through a back door before I could be lynched on the spot, which still happens often. People die to the sounds of screaming crowds over accusations of having profaned the Prophet or the Quran.

In the police van that would bring me back to prison, I was chained like a wild beast, even though I had arrived in the courtroom unbound. But I could read the harshness in the eyes of the officers. I was more worthless to them than an animal. The verdict had turned me into a social leper. I was worse than impure, worse than the devil. I twisted my neck to look through the window in an attempt to find Ashiq's face in the crowd. I knew he was hidden somewhere, not far off. I desperately needed his goodness, love, and support to give me the strength to return to prison.

We had decided during his previous visit to me in prison that he wouldn't attend the trial. It was safer that way. The crowd might lash out at him. He promised to pray for me throughout the whole trial and to stay outside nearby: "Asia, I will be there the whole time. You won't leave my thoughts or my heart. I will also pray for your courage. You will be home soon."

Foolish and so full of confidence, I replied, "Of course we will reunite soon. The judges can only recognize my innocence. I can't wait to hold you and the children in my arms."

Ashiq smiled at me, and his gentle face lit up. "Yes, it's almost over. After a year in that prison, it's finally time for you to come back to us. The children and I are planning a lovely celebration for you. They're overwhelmed with joy at seeing you again. They miss you so much. But we can never go back to Ittan-Walli. It will be sad to lose our house, but it would be too dangerous," Ashiq added, looking defeated. "People in our village see us as pariahs, and it's impossible for us to go back now. All of them threatened me, even our closest neighbors."

"Oh, Ashiq," I said, "the joy of being free and the warmth

of being with my family again are all that matters. Never mind the rest."

We were already picturing our new life—both of us certain that I would be freed soon, and we would put prison far behind us. It calmed our hearts.

Now back in my cell again, I lay face down on the ground for hours. My heart and mind completely empty. I had no tears left. I had already cried all of them out. I turned my head to stare at the dirty wall by the door. I was in a daze when a mocking rat stopped before for me, as if to tell me to pull myself together. I stared back at it.

"Imagine," I said to the rat, "they all want to see me die over something I didn't do. To see me hang from a rope. It's awful! And what's more, I have to pay a fine of three hundred thousand rupees. It would take more than a lifetime to collect that amount of money! Do I have to pay, then, to be buried?"

Lord, why are you testing me like this? I thought. *Give me the strength not to yield. I am entrusting myself into your hands throughout this ordeal. I trust you, but please don't abandon me. Bless me and be the light for Ashiq and our children. Keep our hearts loving and faithful. Do not let doubt overcome us.*

I was innocent, and judges exist to uphold the truth. Shortly before the judge in my case announced his decision, the court officials had me press my thumb onto documents. But since I couldn't read the documents, I had told myself that important people, like judges, could only be on the side of justice and that all of those papers were going to help me get out of prison—and fast. I foolishly believed in the justice of men.

"Little rat, why are men so cruel? Why do they hate those who believe differently than them? You can, after all, be of different faiths and live without hating each other."

Mafia's cries of joy upon hearing my verdict resounded in my ears like the bells of a church. It was as if her life depended on my death. But by condemning me, my accusers became murderers because you don't kill innocent people. That is not what religion teaches. In fact, even though I don't know much about the Quran, I remember that my lawyer, Saif ul-Malook, quoted this verse from the Quran before the Supreme Court: "He who kills an innocent soul is also killing all humanity." [4] By their own faith, I was innocent.

Even without knowing much about the world outside of Pakistan, I had heard on TV that the death penalty no longer existed in many countries because it was deemed barbaric, and in places where it remained, it was reserved for abominable, bloody crimes. At home, the law wanted to kill me, but the death penalty's only accomplishments were making victims out of people who were often innocent and murderers out of judges and those who supported them.

"Most-loving Father, spread your tenderness over my children who no longer have a mommy! Our Father, who art in heaven, I believe in you," I prayed aloud.

---

4   Quran: 5:32.

The rat shook its head from left to right and then froze, as if it were seriously listening to me. At the end of my prayer, it let out a little cry and disappeared through the same hole in the wall from which it had come. This place was slowly killing me. I had been so hopeful to leave it. With my eyes glued to the ceiling, I thought deeply, trying to understand the cruelty of the human heart.

Shortly before my trial, a prosecutor, Muhammad Amin Bokhari, had come to see me in prison. He had a kind face and told me he wanted to help me. He said he was there to prepare for the trial by listening to my version of events. I told the prosecutor about the weeks leading up to the harvest, during which I had fought with the village leader and my neighbor Mafia who, alongside her sister, later accused me of blasphemy.

I had been watching over the water buffalo one day, as I was often used to doing. There were six of them, and in exchange for this work, I would earn one hundred rupees.[5] That day, one of the buffalo lost its mind. It stopped in its tracks and refused to move along with the rest of the herd. I pulled on the braided hemp rope with all my might and even tried to push it, but the more frustrated I got, the more wound up the buffalo became.

Now enraged, the buffalo was uncontrollable. It started to run, and I did everything I could to hold it back with what little strength I had left. I slid on my heels as it charged ahead, and the friction from the rope burned my hands. I had to let go. I

---

5   65 cents (USD)

fell on my behind, scrambled back to my feet, and tried to catch up with it, but it was too late: the animal had destroyed Mafia's wooden trough. She came out of her house, her face full of fury. She shouted at me and told me I would pay for this.

The prosecutor, looking serious, wrote quickly without crossing anything out. I watched the pages of his notebook fill with black ink and felt reassured by his thoroughness. Then, barely lifting up his head, his eyes full of suspicion, he asked, "Did you say anything back to your neighbor?"

"Oh no, sir, I didn't say anything unpleasant. I felt very bad about it. I asked her to forgive me. I even offered to have my husband come and fix the trough. And then I went home, having pocketed the one hundred rupees."

"That's good, Asia. Is there something else you'd like to tell me?"

"No, sir, I've told you everything. I don't know why those women are saying all of this, but I promise I didn't insult anyone. I didn't say anything blasphemous. I respect Muslims, and I have steered clear of such affairs all my life."

I must have spent over an hour telling him about that cursed day and how the rage of the women had been set off over nothing. I explained everything in detail, repeatedly stressing that I had not committed blasphemy. He reassured me with fancy words and a big, calm smile. If I were innocent, he said, then I would be heard. Just before leaving the office in which he had interrogated me, the prosecutor turned around and said, "You did well, speaking up. God is your judge now."

What a joke! The prosecutor was deceitful, and I had been fooled. In fact, I realize now that they were all laying traps for me. From the get-go, they wanted me dead. I walked around and around my little cell, like a cursed goldfish that people threw food at twice a day, as if they needed to fatten me up before they killed me.

Oh! My Ashiq, you must be despairing, I thought. He, too, believed so much that I would be freed. *Where are you? What are you doing? Have you explained this terrible decision to our children? Do they understand that they will never see their mommy again?*

"No attenuating circumstances," the judge had said, meaning he had found no grounds for leniency. But why should I have to supply such grounds? I was innocent; my only wrong in their eyes was that I am a Christian who defended my faith. I would never say a bad thing about another religion. Mafia and her sister had lied, and the *mullah* had believed their embittered gossip.

My deepest nature has since changed. I lost my innocence, and even though I am now free and in a country that wishes me well, I am wary of the kindness of strangers. If someone I don't know speaks kindly to me, I wonder what cruelty they are hiding. I didn't want to be like this, and I regret it, but it is who I have become.

Chapter 4

THE HARVEST

Hatred is the winter of the heart.
Victor Hugo, *The Contemplations*

Thoughts of my family and my death sentence consumed my mind when the sound of knocking on cell doors resounded throughout the prison, as they did every morning, to announce walk-time, during which the guards released prisoners out of their cells to roam the courtyard. It was a tiny distraction that I would later be deprived of for years, as I was eventually condemned to remain confined within four walls, like the little rat that visited me from time to time. Although the rat had more freedom than I did, since it slipped in and out of everywhere.

Khalil wore a smile even meaner than usual that morning, and I didn't feel strong enough to go outside. Khalil never truly spoke to me but merely spit his hateful, spiteful words: "You'll soon be hanging from the end of a rope, and you deserve it.

Christians are dogs, and you are going to pay for having dared to sully our Prophet."

He walked over to me as if to study my face. "Are you going to move or what!" he barked.

I felt weaker than ever. My legs no longer had the strength to carry me. The verdict, the insults, the hatred, the belittling. I didn't want to face further unkindness.

"Can I stay in my cell, please?"

Khalil became enraged. "Who do you think you are? You are nothing, and you have no decisions to make."

His tone hit me like a slap, and hoisting myself out of bed, I tripped and then collapsed. Khalil kicked me hard, forcing me to get up. I was completely exhausted.

Outside, the hot air came over me and felt surprisingly good. It was like breathing in a little bit of life. The other imprisoned women watched me from afar, whispering among themselves. Some of them cast dark looks at me and wouldn't let me come near them. They already knew of my sentence. I had become the black sheep of the prison. Their whispers followed me.

A woman spoke gently to me, "Hello, I'm Bouguina. I just got here. What is your name?"

I lowered my gaze. She really *was* speaking to me. The kindness in her voice brought tears to my eyes. I wasn't used to it anymore. But I also knew that once she found out who I was, she would treat me like the others did.

"My name is Asia. I am a Christian, and I was just sentenced to death for blasphemy. You shouldn't stay near me. The others will make you pay for it."

Bouguina smiled kindly at me. "The others will do what they want anyway," she said. "Are you guilty of blasphemy?"

"God help me, no!" I briefly explained to her how a drink of cold water and the lies of my neighbors had brought me here.

"I am Muslim," said Bouguina, "and I have no problem sharing my dishware with Christian women. That is unfair. Did they really sentence you for that? How is that possible?"

I told Bouguina my story.

My life changed dramatically on June 14, 2009. It was very hot outside, and the earth had cracked from the heat. I had signed up for the big berry-picking harvest to earn a few rupees, like I did every year.

Ashiq worked in a brick-making facility, and Sundays were his only day of rest. His work was so difficult and tiring. I was proud of Ashiq for making bricks. His boss was, too, and every morning he would say to his employees, "You are the pillars of construction work, and thanks to the bricks you make all day long, you are participating in the construction and the grandeur of Pakistan, '*Pakistan zindabad*!'"[6]

That morning, I turned to look at Ashiq, still sound asleep with our two daughters, before heading out the door for the harvest. Moved by the sight of them, I thanked God for giving

---

6   "Long live Pakistan!"

me such a beautiful family. We were not rich, and the 250 rupees I was supposed to earn for this harvest would buy enough flour to make *chapatis* and feed us for an entire week.

When I arrived at the fields, dozens of women were already hard at work. They were crouched down and folded over, their backs bent. With the heat, it looked like it would be a grueling day. A few women poked their heads out of the bushes to nod hello to me, and I recognized Mafia, my neighbor who lived directly across from me. I often saw her through her green gate, stitching away on her old sewing machine in her courtyard amidst her chickens.

A woman in patched-up clothing approached me without hesitation, an empty basin in her hand: "If you fill up the basin, you will get your 250 rupees. But you can only pick the fruits that are red and fully ripe. Otherwise, it doesn't count."

Looking at the enormous container, I thought I would never have time to finish before sunset. I looked at the other women's basins and realized that mine was bigger. It was a way of telling me that as a Christian, I was worth less than the other women. Christians often receive less pay than Muslims for accomplishing the same tasks. Luckily, Ashiq wasn't a victim of this injustice. He earned just as much as the Muslim workers did.

The heat took my breath away. My throat was so dry that I struggled to unglue my lips, and my tongue seemed to double in size. Despite this fever, the rest of the women continued their work without taking a break. Maybe this monotonous, repetitive, and so very meticulous task helped them to forget their thirst?

I walked to the well. The fresh and shiny water sang out to me like a sweet at a party. I took the dented metal cup that was resting on the ledge, filled it with water, and drank large gulps. The cold liquid ran down my throat, and my strength returned little by little. *One more cup to give me some energy*, I thought to myself. I was thinking about how happy I was to be able to improve my family's life with the 250 rupees that I was going to earn. It was so rare! Then I heard hisses of *haram*, which is Arabic for "impure." I understood what that word meant and knew it was aimed at me. My gaze caught Mafia's hateful eyes before she called out to the woman standing near me.

"Don't drink that water," Mafia told her. "It's been soiled now. The Christian woman has filled our cup several times and laid her impure lips on it. Because of her, the water is *haram*, and we can no longer drink it."

The other woman leapt away from me, as if I were going to infect her with a serious illness. I was horrified. Mafia egged the others on, riling them up. I heard angry shouts of *haram* burst from every direction. Why so much malice? I could not understand what I had done to deserve such an attack. It gripped my heart, and I instinctively straightened up to defend myself: "Love one another. That is what Jesus teaches us. I am sure your Prophet Muhammad would agree with him."

My audacity froze my companions before inflaming their

anger even further, which Mafia triggered: "You Christian animal! Your mouth shouldn't even speak the name of the Prophet."

The women began to surround me, screaming, "Your Jesus is just a dog, too, a fatherless bastard. Muhammad had a father named Abdullah, whom he acknowledged. Christians are all worthless and impure. You have soiled our water, and you dare to speak of our Prophet. That is a crime, and if you don't want to pay for it, then you must convert to Islam."

"Leave your husband and marry a Muslim man!" shouted another.

I was dumbstruck. Jesus is full of love, and it hurt to hear him disparaged and insulted in this way.

"Why should I convert to your religion?" I asked. "My faith runs deep, and I refuse to renounce it. Everything you are saying about Jesus is false. My religion teaches us to love everyone, with all our differences. And I am sure your Prophet would agree with that." Carried away by indignation, I poured my heart out and forgot for a moment that I was part of a minority that was supposed to be silent.

The crowd roared like thunder, and when their anger exploded into hatred, the gathering of women threw themselves at me with violence. I was dizzy from the women striking me and spitting on me. I heard their insults and their desire to destroy me: "Dirty woman! You and your family deserve to die and be fed to the pigs. You are nothing, and you dare to speak our Prophet's name. You are going to pay for this!"

Their blows rained down harder and harder. I crumpled to the ground, a ball of pain and sadness.

Bouguina listened to my story in silence. Now she sat still, as if she were ashamed of the behavior of her Muslim brothers and sisters.

"It is painful for me to tell you all this, Bouguina," I said. "I have wanted to erase this episode from my life so much that my memory sometimes fails me. I remember that none of my limbs were spared from their blows, and I still weakly defended myself. But I never said anything bad." I continued with my story.

My stubbornness in refusing to renounce my faith and my husband enraged the women even further, particularly Mafia, who couldn't stop herself and encouraged the other women to hit me. Then, by some miracle that I cannot explain, I managed to escape from their cruel circle. I fled to my home, my eyes full of tears and my heart drowning in sorrow.

Ashiq was oiling a bolt on our garden gate when I fell into his arms, trembling and unable to speak through sobs. His gentleness and patience allowed me to slowly calm down and tell him everything: my thirst, the dented cup, the unfair accusations of having rendered the water impure, the insults, the blows. The words spilled out, and I could not have imagined the hellish chain of events that would follow.

Now I look back at who I was at the time and feel guilty for having put my family through all of this. Should I have been silent? Were a cup of water and a display of pride worth those years of suffering? Of course, if I had known the consequences, I would have let them say whatever they wanted. I wouldn't have opened my mouth. But on the other hand, I am proud that I held firmly to my Christianity. I remained strong and loyal to my faith. Doesn't God often test those he loves?

Ashiq cradled me like a child for a long time after I told him what had happened at the harvest. His words took my sorrow away: "Forget about it. I'm sure they will forget it by tomorrow and move on to something else."

His tenderness and my tears washed my soul, even if I could still hear the hateful words of the women echo in my ears. The tears and shock finally got the better of my exhausted body, and I fell asleep to the sound of his comforting words.

"Your story is horrible, Asia," Bouguina said when I paused to reflect. "And they sentenced you to death for that?" Her outrage was genuine. In this cruel world, it did so much good to speak with someone like Bouguina, who understood the injustice of the awful experience. I pressed on.

The day after they attacked me at the well, the women told the village *mullah*'s wife that I had said blasphemous things about Islam. The *mullah* announced this over the mosque's loudspeakers, ensuring everyone knew. The villagers gathered around my house, shouting that I needed to convert. After five days, the village *mullah*, alongside Mafia and her sister, came and found me in my own house. Mafia, with a smug look on her face, shouted, "She has to be dragged through the whole village like a filthy animal, with a rope around her neck!"

The enraged crowd dragged me into the home of a Muslim neighbor. Then an elegant young man, his chin lined with a long black beard, burst into the house's little courtyard. It was the *mullah* of my village, who said, "I was told you had insulted our Prophet. Is this true?"

"I beg you!" I implored him. "I didn't do anything! I didn't say anything!"

The *mullah* turned to Mafia: "Did she speak ill of Muslims and of our holy Prophet Muhammad?"

"Yes, she was insulting," Mafia retorted, "but I can't repeat what she said. Otherwise I would be committing blasphemy in turn."

"It's true. She insulted our religion," her sister added.

"Please, I didn't say anything bad about the Prophet. I just refused to convert. I am allowed to keep my own religion."

"Asia committed a serious sin!" Mafia exclaimed. "That day, she said terrible things about Islam. We didn't try to convert her. She got angry because we pointed out to her that she shouldn't have been drinking out of our cup."

"It's because she's Christian," her sister then cried out. "Religion forbids us to drink out of the same cup as her!"

In the middle of my story, I turned to Bougina and said, "You are Muslim. Is it true that I soiled the cup?"

"Muslims here don't like to share their dishware with Christians. It isn't written in the Quran, and it is bad to behave that way. But *mullahs*, in general, don't oppose them, because it is a cultural taboo. People would accuse them of being *infidels.*" I understood then that Bouguina's words must have been true. I was nearing the end of my story, or at least the part that landed me in prison and sitting next to Bouguina.

When I tried to defend myself, the *mullah* had shouted, "You are lying! Everyone says you committed blasphemy. That is sufficient proof. Christians must obey Pakistani law, which forbids any disparaging remarks about the holy Prophet. Since the Prophet cannot defend himself, we are going to avenge him and file a complaint at the police station unless you convert to Islam."

Then two policemen arrived. They threw me into their van amid the cheers of the angry village. A few minutes later, I was in the Nankana Sahib police station and standing across from a policeman. The *mullah*, Mafia, and other women had already told the chief of police that I had insulted the Prophet.

The policeman wrote out the official report and turned to me: "What do you have to say about all this? Were you blasphemous?"

"No, I wasn't blasphemous."

"You admit you were blasphemous?"

"I am innocent. Take pity on me! I am asking for your forgiveness."

"Accept Islam and you will go free. Marry another and you will be free. Leave your family and you will be free," the policeman rambled on.

"No, no, I don't want to leave my family or change religions."

"Too bad for you. The complaint has been filed, and justice will decide. While you await your trial, you will go to Sheikhupura prison."

I later learned that my two daughters had also been beaten and forced to drink urine. It was atrocious.

"Oh Asia, your story makes me shiver," Bouguina said. "I feel outraged by it." Her tone, a mixture of gentleness and indignation, warmed my heart. Finally, someone understood.

I took her two hands vigorously into mine and muttered, "Thank you."

It was already time to go back to our cells. The bell rang, and the guard pushed us unceremoniously back inside. Bouguina smiled and shook my hands: "Asia, stay hopeful. God will not abandon you. You aren't dead yet, and anything can happen. Prayer is a light."

I watched her heading away, happy to have found a friend in this place that was almost hell. You were right, Bouguina. Anything could happen. It took ten years, but I am free now. I am with my dear Ashiq and my children. I never thought that it would be possible. Now far from Pakistan, I think back to your words, Bouguina. You gave me the first glimmer of hope. I will never forget you.

Chapter 5

TO BE CHRISTIAN IN PAKISTAN

Minorities are allowed to be wrong. They are violent, and why?
Because they are weak. Majorities are condemned to always being right.
VICTOR HUGO, *THINGS SEEN*

Prior to being thrown into prison, I hardly knew anything outside my village. In my world, Christians rarely attend school. I grew up in the countryside, and all I saw were fields and my Muslim neighbors working them. I am not educated, but I quickly understood that they were no more informed than I was. They knew the Quran, and I knew the Bible.

In my experience, Islamists are mean but not exclusively toward Christians. Muslims, too, fear the Islamists. It is important to understand that Islamism is a political ideology, not a form of the Muslim faith. They are not representative of Pakistani people, and they are not seen on every street corner, but they dictate their will to Parliament. The Islamists and their influence are terrible because everybody fears them—even the ministers and the president. Everyone feels helpless because the Islamists aren't afraid to lay down bombs or ally with the Taliban to kill others and themselves in Allah's name. In fact, I think the judges who sentenced me to death in the Nankana Court and High Court of Lahore must have been scared of them too.

I am proud to be Christian. Apparently, we make up less than two percent of the population in Pakistan. Even though we are not considered a threat, we aren't respected either. Most people are wary of us because we don't believe in Allah, and the Christian community suffers from all sorts of disdain. That attitude has always been anchored in people's minds. We have to state our religion on our identification papers, and our passport has a different color: black. Before anyone opens it, they already know we are Christians. It's as if we have a mark in the middle of our faces, and in Pakistan, this mark is not an asset. The vast majority of Christians are limited to cleaning the streets, and we are called *choori,* an extremely demeaning, even insulting, nickname that basically means "a person who cleans the toilets." In the countryside, it is difficult for us to own land because Muslims refuse to sell their seeds to us at a reasonable price. For us, seeds are much more expensive.

Even though there are many good Christian schools, they are too expensive for most of us. And it is often Muslims who study there! I was not able to go to school because my family was too poor, but it was important to me that my children knew how to read and write and for them to find good jobs. I don't want people calling them *choori.* Ashiq and I talked about this a lot, and we agreed that our children would go to school, even though it meant making sacrifices. The school they attended was a miserable building with hardly any furniture or equipment, but they learned so much. Still, I feared for them. Every day, their classmates would encourage them to convert to Islam and sometimes insult or push them around if our daughters said they believed in Jesus or were proud of their religion.

One day, my Sidra, who is deeply sensitive, came home shaken. At the boy's school next to hers, a fifteen-year-old Christian named Sharoon was severely beaten and died from his injuries. Sharoon was a very good student, and for daring to be so, a whole group of kids abused him for months and months. All of the adults turned a blind eye, and the police refused to recognize that he had been harassed for being a Christian. Sharoon's brothers were so afraid that the same thing would happen to them that they no longer wanted to attend school. Sidra couldn't stop crying, and all I could do to console her was hug her tightly. Life for Christians in Pakistan is hard enough; why must even children be mean to them at school? Christian students lose bonus points to Muslim students who are able to recite the Quran. Even the textbooks they study have insulting, false things written about Christians and other minorities. Sidra once read a passage to me that described Christians as inferior, bad people who should be treated as enemies and whom others should be wary of.

Thankfully, schools in Canada treat all of their students equally. The students are taught to be kind to everyone and to respect all religions. They can study in safety and in peace. I am very proud of my children's success. They will become teachers, doctors, or maybe even lawyers! That is what my daughter, Eisham, wants to do. She will work hard at it.

In Pakistan's major cities, Christians live differently from those who live in the countryside. They live in certain neighborhoods, which some call ghettos. Once a year, Ashiq, the children, and I would travel to a neighborhood in Lahore to celebrate Easter at the Joseph Colony, a Christian community that was built on marshland. Trash lines the muddy ground, and the air is saturated with black dust spat out by the neighboring factories. The people have never welcomed non-Christians, but we had friends, Chazia and Akbar, among the 450 Christians who lived there, crowded into little buildings. Chazia and Akbar would invite us to share an Easter meal. They and their three little ones had big hearts.

In 2013, I feared for Chazia and Akbar. During one of Ashiq's visits to me in prison, he told me that the entire Joseph Colony was the target of a neighboring mob, a turbulent crowd of people whipped into a frenzy by religious extremists. These mobs are willing to destroy everything in the name of Islam, and they are what we Christians fear most. More than 150 homes had been destroyed in the Joseph Colony following a fight between a Muslim and a Christian. A Muslim man had accused Sawan Masih, a Christian, of blasphemy, and during Friday prayers at the mosque, Muslim leaders called for an immediate protest. A crowd converged on the colony to burn everything, using accelerants to ensure the complete destruction of homes and small churches. At the time, Ashiq's words had reassured me because Chazia and Akbar's family was unharmed, and the government had agreed to pay for the repairs. As for Sawan Masih, the man who was accused of blasphemy for no reason, I believe he is still waiting to die in prison.

This has happened to other people, like Shakil, a Christian woman from the village next to mine, and her son, Izhan, who was only nine years old. Her Muslim neighbors couldn't stand the fact that little Izhan played with their children, so they accused him of having burned the Quran. The police arrested both mother and son without bothering to check whether the accusation was true. Both were beaten and faced the death penalty. Fortunately, an organization of people who protect the innocent from injustice made so much noise and attracted so much attention that Shakil and Izhan were freed. Still, this mob was ready to murder a nine-year-old child because he played with Muslims. Just thinking about it sends a chill through my heart.

Often, in fact, mobs are so electrified with hatred that they don't wait for a judge to return a verdict. Such was the case for Shazad and Shama Masih, a Christian couple with three children.

Shazad and Shama worked in a village near our home and were accused of dirtying the Quran. Their neighbors called the police, but they were too late. A hostile crowd of hundreds upon hundreds of people descended upon them like an enormous wave. The mob—their rage inhuman—beat Shazad and Shama before burning them alive, leaving their children orphans.

My painful experience taught me that politics and religion don't go together well. And when you are part of a minority, you are more vulnerable to acts of stupidity and hatred. The penalties for crimes are doubled because we are despised, and treatment is even worse for women. Young Christian women are often abducted, kept by force, and raped, sometimes by multiple men. The women are forced to convert to Islam and then married without any say in the matter. If they dare to resist, they risk being burned with acid or killed. If they make it out alive, they are shattered for the rest of their lives.

This tragedy befell Asma Yaqoob, the twenty-five-year-old daughter of Yaqoob Masih, a Christian from our community. Asma was gentle and lovely as the dawn. She worked for a Muslim family that treated her rather well. Muhammad Rizwan Gujjar, a Muslim man, had decided that he wanted to marry her. Asma had no desire to marry him, and she didn't want to convert to Islam. She resisted for many weeks, refusing his proposals, which enraged the young man. Fortunately, Asma's employer, Saeeduz Zaman, was a good man who supported and protected her, but it wasn't enough. One day, Asma answered a knock on the door of her home. Yaqoob heard her howling in pain, and when he found her, Gujjar was standing over her and watching flames devour her body. Gujjar killed her. Asma suffered an excruciating death because she refused to marry him. Gujjar was arrested, but Yaqoob lost his daughter forever. The poor man has since lost his senses. How could anyone recover from such a tragedy?

I don't understand the madness of humanity, and I don't understand how such evil, harmful, and unjust laws can exist. How can people put someone to death and believe it a good thing? How can they turn children into orphans so pitilessly? How can anyone believe that God delights in such cruelty? What world do we live in?

At first, the court's emphasis on my religion led me to believe that the anti-blasphemy laws were only aimed at the Christian community. It took me years to understand that it also targets Muslims, and deep down, everyone is terrified of it. All one must do is fight with a neighbor to wind up sentenced to death or life in prison. Christians and Muslims both live in gripping fear that someone with ill intentions might wrongfully accuse them, and that is exactly what happened to me. From the depths of my cell, I realized that hundreds of us waited for our deaths, trapped between stone walls, over accusations of crimes that were rarely, if ever, actually committed.

Amidst all these horrors, though, are glimmers of hope, and I am bold enough to believe that my story has contributed to them. In March 2018, the Pakistani Senate's Special Commission on Human Rights approved the decision to severely punish any accusation of blasphemy that is false or fabricated to prevent people from using this law indiscriminately. If the accuser wants to press charges, he or she will need at least two witnesses to support the accusation. Of course, finding fake witnesses isn't difficult, and the anger of those on the streets remains a dangerous thing, but it is heartwarming to see that my country is fighting for more justice, less cruelty, and a bit more respect.

People are also standing up to defend the victims of injustice. People like Jacqueline Sultan, a lawyer who fights for the rights of minorities and against the forced conversions of young girls. But Jacqueline, like almost everyone else fighting these types of injustice, receives death threats almost every day. Not so long ago, a lawyer named Rizvam was defending a Christian in a blasphemy lawsuit, and the prosecutor launched himself at Rizvam in the middle of the courtroom, brutally attacking and beating him. The violence of the blows was such that other lawyers had to intervene and rush Rizvam to the hospital. He was severely wounded and almost lost his sight. And yet, the prosecutor's violence didn't seem to bother the judge, who simply left the courtroom. In a court of law, a judge is supposed to seek out and uphold justice, not be complicit in such barbarous acts. One must pray again and again that God will protect those who fight these absurd laws.

In the summer of 2018, the election of Imran Khan as prime

minister gave all of Pakistan's minorities a great deal of hope. He promised to protect persecuted Christians and the oppressed. Finally we had a leader who considered us and recognized that we are all entitled to the same amount of respect. He defended me personally by celebrating my acquittal and throwing into jail all the protesters who continued to demand my death.

Despite these kinds of victories, Pakistan has much to do. Will Khan remove the false, offensive illustrations of Christians and other minorities from schoolbooks? Will he force the Pakistani authorities to allow Christians to secure jobs that match their skill levels? Will he dare to take action against the blasphemy law? In my sordid dungeon, his election brought hope to my heart. Anne-Isabelle explained to Ashiq and me that I had a better chance of making it out alive with a prime minister like Imran Khan than I had with Nawaz Sharif,[7] a man who was close to the Islamists and who, as prime minister, called for the death of those accused of committing blasphemy against the Prophet.

God heard our prayers and breathed some common sense into people. Now, I am safe and alongside my family, but I worry that the Islamists will seek revenge on my Christian brothers and sisters because of me. Despite the difficulties and injustices, I miss my country. I was happy to lead a simple life among my own in Ittan-Walli, and I was sad to have to leave in order to escape

---

7   Prime Minister of Pakistan from 1990 to 1993, from 1997 to 1999, and from 2013 to 2017.

death's clutches. I would so very much like for life as a Christian in Pakistan to no longer be a problem and for us to be treated the same as Muslims. One must never stop believing and hoping.

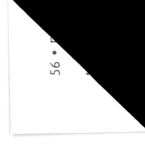

Chapter 6

THE POPES

Christians and Muslims have generally misunderstood each other,
and sometimes, in the past, we have opposed each other
and even exhausted ourselves with polemics and wars.
I think God welcomes us, today, to change our old habits.
POPE JOHN PAUL II, SPEECH, 1985

People often wonder why and how I became famous around
the world. They forget that it is thanks to Pope Benedict XVI.
I first learned of the pope's intervention during Ashiq's visit to
me after the white-bearded judge had sentenced me to hang. I
had not seen Ashiq in over a year, and it was a visit I will always
remember.

Usually, I was able to tell day from night because silence
rules over the latter. But in prison, all points of reference are
disrupted. Without thinking about it and without meaning to be,
I was always on alert. The slightest movement or noise would
wake me at night or make me jump during the day. When the

ame came to sleep, I remained awake and rolled up into a ball under my blanket. Day and night, I dozed off from time to time without ever feeling like I was fully asleep. Often, the prison's sounds would pull me out of those dreamless sleeps.

In fact, once I was sentenced to death, I quit dreaming—no doubt because I subconsciously understood that life was now behind me. I had been rotting away for more than a year, and the noises had become familiar to me. The slamming of a door meant the changing of a guard. The jangle of keys and the watchman's footsteps, mixed with the groaning wheels of the soup cart, meant mealtime. A metal bucket dragging along the hallway tiles meant the evening chore...or was it the morning chore?

After my sentencing, I felt myself slowly dying. Painlessly, for the time being, but slowly. I was no longer capable of expressing what I felt. Fear, for sure, but I was less frightened than I had been at the start of my ordeal. For the first few days, the fear beat inside my chest like a drum, but then it calmed down. I jumped less. I did not sob as much, but the tears still fell from my eyes regularly. In a way, my tears were the first witnesses to the injustice that had befallen me and were my only companions in my cell. My life was one of suffering, but my tears reminded me that I hadn't completely given up.

The Nankana Court had thrown me into the depths of this humid, cold cell, so small that I could touch both walls if I stretched out my arms. However, the real challenge was not prison but being deprived of my own children—my reason for living. The court revoked my right to see them, and I mourned their absence every day. Not being able to touch them, hear their songs, or enjoy their love of life. Instead, my memories of them played like a soft melody. I missed my small but lovely, full life. Throughout those long years of separation, I would tirelessly tell myself that I would give everything I had to be at home with my daughters for a moment, cuddling up with them. Even when I am with my daughters today, it hurts to think back to the pain of separation and what they must have felt. How brutal it was. They were too young to be thrown into the cruel world of adults.

On the day I found out Pope Benedict XVI knew who I was, I had been shivering from the cold under my thin, worn blanket. Winter was approaching. In our small house in Ittan-Walli, we didn't have heat during the two months of winter. Instead, I would snuggle up to Ashiq for his body heat. His body, whether it was summer or winter, day or night, was always warm. He would wrap his arms around me on cold nights and rest his chin on top of my head. In those moments, I didn't realize how loved and protected he made me feel.

Ten days after the farce that was my first trial, I was sitting in my bed in pain, feeling as if I were a hundred years old. Then I heard quick, impatient steps coming down the hall. The footsteps stopped outside my door. Silence.

My heart pounded in my chest. Given the judge's fatal verdict, I could find myself with a rope around my neck at any moment. I wasn't afraid of death; I know that whenever it happens, God on high will be standing there at the end of my journey to greet me with a smile. But I was afraid of dying.

Certain these were my final moments, I curled up and held my breath. My heart stopped beating. I couldn't hear anything anymore. Then, I joined my hands together, closed my eyes, and began to pray, whispering, "My God, save me. Lord Jesus, how do I pray well when evil crushes me? I can take it no longer. You who experienced the greatest depths of suffering, you who have been through this, be with me today. You who were able to cope until the end, help me hold on. You who are alive, pray in me through your Holy Spirit. And while I go through this ordeal, fill me with the breath of your resurrection."

The cell door opened abruptly to Khalil's furious, menacing face: "Hurry up, we're leaving!"

From my bed, I lowered my eyes to the ground and whispered, "Where are we going?"

"Who gave you permission to ask questions, you filthy worm? Get a move on. I've got other things to do!"

I jumped. My whole body trembled, and he seemed to enjoy the sight of my terror. Raving mad, Khalil stomped toward me, threatening to beat me, and with one big kick, he knocked the bed over and me with it. I scrambled to my feet and followed him out of my cell. The doors to the other cells were open and empty. I quickly realized we weren't on our way to the exercise area. I hobbled along, like a well-raised animal, following this man without knowing where he was taking me.

Khalil led me into a small room with chairs. It was the prison's visitation room! What a relief. Other prisoners were already fully immersed in conversations with their families. I saw Bouguina, who gave me a small, friendly wave, but I restlessly wondered who was visiting me. Hope reignited within me when I saw Ashiq standing in the doorway! Behind our smiles lay enormous sorrow. Ashiq managed to hold back his tears, but I could not.

"Tell me, how are our children doing?" I begged. "And why aren't they with you?"

Ashiq assured me that they were safe and told me it would be too dangerous for them to come to prison. Then, with an impish smile, he held out a plastic bag. "The girls and I are managing very well. They made you a surprise: the *chapatis* you love so much."

I pressed them to my heart, thinking of how they had flattened out the dough with their small hands. "I am so happy and proud that they know how to make the bread without me. Let them know that, Ashiq." In my nine years of detainment, my daughters came to see me only three times. My sweet, innocent children were also receiving death threats from extremists. Worry for my daughters turned into panic, and tears ran down my face.

"Where are you living? How do you manage to feed yourselves since you lost your job?"

Ashiq tried to reassure me with his words, patting the back of my hand. "My Asia, I came here to bring you good news, so I beg you to dry your tears and listen to me. We're going to appeal your death sentence. Governor Salman Taseer has found you a lawyer, and the Minister of Minorities, Shahbaz Bhatti, has loaned us a house in Lahore. He is paying for it. We will be safe there because nobody knows where we are."

"What about our house in Ittan-Walli?"

"For now, your sister and her husband are holding on to it, but it is hard for them to stay there. They are going to have to abandon it to avoid being beaten to death."

I knew I was innocent, but I felt guilty for having destroyed the lives of my family. I started sobbing again. Ashiq wiped away my tears, and I fought back my cries as best as I could and stifled another sob.

"Calm down, Asia, I haven't finished. I have more good news."

With a smile on the corner of his lips, Ashiq pulled out a piece of newspaper and showed me a woman's picture. "You see this woman? She is a Western journalist who has decided to help us. I told her you are innocent, and she wants to meet you. So when she comes, you have to tell her everything."

I examined the picture of the stranger's face. It reminded me of something. "You know that animal we have seen several times on TV? The one with the long neck...What's it called again?"

"Oh yes, I forget, but you're right. She is tall and thin in real life."

We laughed heartily—the way we used to. The feeling was both familiar and new to me.

"But you know, Asia, that's not all. You'll never guess who spoke of you. Do you want to know?" he asked, teasing me.

"Oh, yes! Tell me quickly, please!"

Ashiq inhaled deeply once more and then took the plunge: "Pope Benedict XVI talked about you on Saint-Peter's Square in Rome, Italy."

I jumped for joy in my chair and cried out, "You're kidding!?"

A guard motioned at me to calm down. I sat back in my chair to avoid having the visit cut short. "Tell me about it," I said to Ashiq in a hushed tone. "How is that possible? I can't believe the pope talked about me!"

"Well, I don't really know. Maybe Minister Shahbaz Bhatti told him about you. They know each other. Or maybe it's because I have answered a lot of questions from foreign journalists since the court's decision. Plus, you know, you are the first and only woman who has been sentenced to death in Pakistan in the course of this century, so everyone is taking an interest in you."

"But do you know what he said exactly?"

"Yes."

"Go on, tell me!"

Ashiq smiled at my impatience. "He said, in front of thousands of people and on TV: 'I am thinking of Asia Bibi and her family, and I ask that she be given her freedom as soon as possible,' adding that he also prayed for all Christians in Pakistan, who are often subject to violence and discrimination."

I could only let out a long breath. I had no words.

"You know, he talked about us too. He said, 'Asia Bibi and her family.'"

"That is amazing! All is not lost then. We have to keep faith. Our Lord is with us, and he is going to get me out of here."

"Of course you're going to get out of here. Tell me about you. How are you? How are the other inmates treating you?"

I looked around at the families and realized that we, the prisoners, didn't have all that much to say. Inside of prisons, things run in circles.

"Everyone hates me here except Bouguina. Look, that's her in the back next to the radiator. She is Muslim and—"

"Visit's over!" thundered Khalil.

Ashiq shook my hand and gave me a gentle look. "Have faith. Remain hopeful. I will be back soon."

Back in my cell, my heart felt lighter. That night, for the first time, I fell asleep with a warm heart. The governor of the province, the minister, the journalist, and the pope himself! He was thinking of me and praying for me, and I wondered if I deserved that honor and attention. I still wonder it today because Pope Francis has also expressed dismay at my situation. I am a simple farm girl, and so many people are suffering on earth.

In 2013, I received an award in Madrid for freedom of conscience against intolerance and fanaticism. The whole family was invited on a trip, and it was amazing for them. They were even able to meet Anne-Isabelle, who worked to have the distinction awarded to me. The trip was a breath of fresh air for them since their daily lives were horrible: always in hiding and living in constant fear of being seen. In my country, everybody spies on and fears each other. Pakistanis are no more evil than other human beings, but they are afraid, and fear often reveals the lowest instincts. I blamed myself for causing my family so much grief, so I was happy they could feel the love and compassion of strangers and benefit from our pain in some way. Otherwise, Ashiq and my daughters would never have seen anything beyond Pakistani lands.

With the news of the pope's prayers and support, I suddenly wasn't afraid of death; I was more afraid of life. When Ashiq told me about their stay in Spain and receiving the prize, which acknowledged my bravery and brought worldwide attention to my wrongful imprisonment, I immediately wanted our family to write a letter to Pope Benedict XVI:

> January 24, 2013
>
> To everyone concerned about my fate, particularly Pope Benedict XVI, I ask you to consider sharing your love and support with everyone abroad who is helping me. I am grateful for all of your prayers.
>
> Pope Benedict XVI, thanks to your prayers, my husband was able to visit Madrid in Spain. I am very proud that he was able to receive a prize in my name. It is a great honor for us to be Christians. I have been in prison for over four years now. My faith remains very strong and after having received the

prize, I am even stronger than I was before. Because I am in prison, I entrust to you my children and husband, who will be safe in your prayers. You are the greatest guardian of my family.

These last few days, I have fallen ill, and if I lose my life, please take care of my daughters, Eisha and Eisham, and ensure that they are healthy and receive a good education. I want them to be well-brought-up girls in society. Here in prison, I feel weaker and weaker. I love my daughters very much. Please take care of them.

I thank you for your support, and I urgently beseech you to be kind enough to do something to help me gain my freedom as soon as possible. I would like to be able to see those I love again, with my eyes open, before I die. I pray for peace, and I would like to live with my family in peace among you all.

—Asia Bibi

After this letter was published and relayed to international press, Anne-Isabelle scolded Ashiq. She said that if we called upon the pope, then I wouldn't have a chance of making it out of jail. We had a hard time understanding this because, in our minds, the support of the pope could hurt no one. I eventually understood when Anne-Isabelle explained it to me in person when she came to see me in Canada years later. I also understand now why I became a symbol for the anti-blasphemy laws. When the pope comes to your defense, Islamists see it as a duel between Islam and the Catholic Church. My life was caught between the two faiths.

I became the Christian who was to be put to death no matter what it took. I also found out that after the Vatican took that position, hateful protests broke out throughout the country. The fundamentalists and religious parties promised chaos if I wasn't hanged in the coming days. In the crowds of angry men, some brandished photographs of Pope Benedict XVI, while others swung nooses around in the air. A *mullah* even promised a fifty thousand-rupee reward[8] to whoever killed Asia Bibi. I risked being murdered even within the prison.

Anne-Isabelle brought her computer when she came to see me in Canada, and she read aloud a letter that she had sent to Pope Francis:

> Very Holy Father,
>
> I solemnly request that you interfere in the Asia Bibi affair—the woman who has been sentenced to death in Pakistan—only by associating with your Muslim counterparts...I know you are sympathetic to the fate of this poor mother of two. I don't mean to offend you or question your authority, but if you intervene, it could reinforce the hatred of the fundamentalists, who are pressuring the Pakistani

8   323 dollars (USD).

government, when our only hope is that she be granted a presidential pardon or that the judges at the Supreme Court have mercy on her.

A week after the initial death sentencing of Asia Bibi on November 17, 2010, Pope Benedict XVI put out this call: "The international community is closely following and preoccupied by the delicate situation of Christians in Pakistan, who are often subject to violence and discrimination. I would particularly like to express my spiritual solidarity with Asia Bibi and her family, and I ask that she be freed promptly." These words of Benedict XVI's were very poorly received in Pakistan. The radical religious parties immediately began demonstrating in several major cities.

I witnessed one of these demonstrations in Lahore, where thousands of people were shouting away that the pope shouldn't be getting involved in their business. I saw a crowd aggressively burn an effigy of the pope while brandishing pictures of Asia Bibi with a noose around her neck. Just after Pope Benedict XVI intervened, the Minister of Minorities Shahbaz Bhatti confided to me: "The situation is really critical now. In the minds of Pakistani radicals, the Catholic Church has infringed upon Islam. They are going to use Asia to get redress."

As a journalist, it is my duty to provide an account

of the complexity of the situation. The Christian community has never abandoned Asia Bibi, and I am deeply thankful for that. But if we want to save Asia Bibi, if that is truly the goal, then we mustn't risk reinforcing the antagonisms between Christians and Muslims.

The Pakistani government is aware of the excessive scale of this affair. Asia Bibi should, of course, never have been sentenced to death. And even if the government or Pakistani courts hear the messages coming from Western diplomacy, they cannot ignore the immense pressure of the Islamists, who make things such that neither the government nor the courts are free.

We have to push all three of the great monotheistic religions to the fore if we want to save Asia Bibi. The time will come when we will be able to denounce the injustices perpetuated against oppressed Christians around the whole world and to question certain abusive laws.

The President of Pakistan, Mamnoon Hussain, has just acknowledged Malala's Nobel Prize. It is up to us to bolster him in his opposition to fundamentalism, rather than to ask him to intervene in the name of Christianity.

Yours sincerely,

Anne-Isabelle Tollet

We laughed a lot when we realized that on the one hand, my family and Christian nongovernmental organizations (NGOs) were doing everything they could to get the pope to intervene on my behalf. On the other, he was being asked not to speak up. The pope must have been lost. In fact, he had the following response sent to Anne-Isabelle:

> January 12, 2015
> Ma'am,
>
> You mentioned in a letter from last October 29, which you sent to the Holy Father, the case of Asia Bibi, a convict in Pakistan.
>
> In the name of His Holiness, I thank you for your comments, which I have duly made note of. As you know, the Holy See continues to closely monitor the situation of Christians in Pakistan and to discuss it regularly with the civil authority through our diplomatic channels.
>
> Rest assured that I pray for your person and your work, Ma'am.
>
> Yours sincerely,
> Mgr. Antoine Camilleri
> Undersecretary for State Relations

Ashiq, the children, and I now understood why the pope had said nothing more about me for years: "I thank you for your comments, which I have duly taken note of." Time passed,

and under pressure from Christian NGOs who were equally surprised at his silence about me, the pope gave us the honor of
granting Ashiq and Eisham a private audience, less than a year
before my release. He said that I "was a model for a society that,
these days, is ever more afraid of pain. Asia Bibi is a martyr." He
gave them a small Bible for me, and it has never left my side.

"I think of your mother very often, and I pray for her,"
Pope Francis added to Eisham.

I was proud of my daughter, who was so grown-up. She
was barely nine years old when I was thrown into jail, and when
I was freed, I found that a young woman of nineteen years had
replaced her. She spoke so well on my behalf and gave interviews
regularly. She asked me to listen to a recording on her smart-
phone of what she said on the radio, and I was so impressed:
"Asia Bibi feels mentally and physically well. She will soon be
freed because we are fighting for her freedom. Even though she
has been suffering for the nine years that she has been in prison,
we hope to obtain her freedom as soon as possible. When she
is freed, she will certainly not be able to survive by remaining in
Pakistan because a lot of people over there are calling for her to
be hanged, despite the whole world's prayers. As soon as she is
freed, she will go somewhere safe and sound immediately."

And my little Eisham was right. I thank heaven every day
for allowing me to live in a calm and peaceful environment far
from Islamist fury. I don't understand how people can be so
hateful out of love for their faith. What I do know, though, is

that the hateful bear traces of deep sadness on their faces. I know that religion can spread terror and even kill. I also know that I became a prisoner of fanaticism in spite of myself. Despite being free, I remain afraid. I know people are still trying to kill me and that the anger of the Islamists will only be appeased once they feel avenged. I know that, even far from Pakistan, they could find me and make me disappear.

Chapter 7

MY SUPPORTERS AND THE PRICE TO BE PAID

People speak sometimes of the bestial cruelty of man,
but that is a terrible insult to the beasts.
FYODOR DOSTOEVSKY, THE BROTHERS KARAMAZOV

In prison, I often saw death coming and knew my days were numbered. I witnessed sudden, brutal disappearances several times, including a particular night of horror that haunts my memory.

A scream jolted me awake, but I couldn't see anything beyond the deep, almost blinding darkness. I had no notion of time or space, but as I lay on my *charpai*,[9] the coldness of my cell reminded me that I was very much awake. I listened carefully but heard nothing other than the calm murmur of the night. *Maybe I dreamt it*, I thought.

Suddenly, a second scream rang out only to fade again.

---

9   *Charpai*: a traditional bed made of braided rope.

Then, a series of moans made me freeze in silence when I realized the groaning was coming from the cell next to mine. It was Bouguina. My tender neighbor was howling to death. Her screams spread panic throughout my body. They echoed against the walls and seemed to push against the bars of my cell. No one reacted, not even the night guards. It was as if I were the only person who heard her cries in the night.

"Bouguina, Bouguina, what is happening?" I screamed, trying to help her.

"Help...need...doctor..."

I could barely make out her words; they were all so broken up. But I understood that it was an emergency. It sounded as though she was twisting in agony. Between two screams, I heard her vomit. My voice was not powerful, but it was loaded with fright: "Help! Help!"

In distress, I banged my fists against the thick wooden door to my cell but heard only the hopeless screams of my friend. I grabbed my scrap iron bowl and banged it against the metal bed legs of my *charpai* to attract the attention of the guards. I felt like I was making an outrageous amount of noise, but nothing happened. No reaction. It was as if Bouguina and I were alone in this prison and in the world. Later, I understood that nobody cared to react. They pretended not to hear.

"Bouguina! Bouguina, talk to me!"

Bouguina did not respond. Then, to my great despair, she stopped crying out. I paced around my cell like a lion in a zoo, hoping Bouguina had fallen asleep. "Bouguina, wake up. Tell me you're doing better!"

Silence. I listened for my dear friend all night long without ever hearing a response. The echoes of her suffering rang in my head until dawn. In the morning, I walked down the little steps that led to the exercise courtyard. As always, all of the other prisoners were already there. I walked over to a small group of young women playing with a cricket ball.

"Excuse me, I'm wondering if my mind isn't playing tricks on me. I heard screams in the night. Did you too?"

Without even considering my question, they turned away from me, yawning and whispering with knowing looks. I stepped aside and went looking for Bouguina. I scoured the small court-yard with my eyes, but it was in vain. I thought she might be in the infirmary. Then an old, wrinkly woman sitting on a low wall snapped coldly, "If it's Bouguina you're looking for, you aren't likely to find her. She died in the night."

"What? No, no! What happened?"

"Someone put poison in her dish. That happens, some-times, you know."

"She can't be dead. That isn't fair. Why would they do that?"

"Who knows."

"I wasn't able to find out why Bouguina was in jail. She was always taking an interest in me. She was so gentle and kind."

"Like a lot of prisoners here, she was raped. The law states that any extramarital relations constitute *zina*, the sin of adultery. She was naïve enough to file a complaint after she was raped by a neighbor, and ultimately, she's the one who got five years of time."

"That's unfair! And why are you here, what did you do?"

"I have been here for twenty years because I killed my husband."

"Oh..."

"Well, I never liked the guy. One night, he tried to spray me with acid. I knew he was going to do it one day. He threatened me repeatedly."

"But why?"

"Oh, trifling business. He felt I wasn't under his thumb enough, so he wanted to teach me a good lesson. Except that night, when I heard him come into my bedroom, I was ready for him. Before he could try anything, I hit him on the head with the machete we used to cut sugar cane stems."

I was shocked.

"Don't get that look on your face, girl. He got what he deserved, and my life is much better now that I am in prison. What about your husband?"

"Oh, my husband is a good and generous man, and—"

DRING!

As all the women headed promptly for the exit door, the old woman whispered, "If I were you, Asia, I would be careful what I ate."

I shivered with dread, realizing that, even in prison, I could be killed. Back in my cell, I felt the loss of Bouguina and how it would deepen my isolation even more. At times, I had dark thoughts and lost all hope. Being locked away and far from my family for nine years, oscillating between hope and despair, I felt my death was certain. And it was a close call. I almost gave up and allowed the grave to take me.

When I learned of the deaths of the governor and the minister shortly thereafter, I was tempted to give up. I felt the bars on my prison cell surround me more closely and the walls close in. I was suffocating, and suicide seemed like a deliverance. I could disappear to save my husband and children. I admit that I thought about it—but not for long. I had no right to abandon my daughters who, throughout all those years, waited for their mother to come home, and they were right to believe so. Now, I savor each new moment I get to spend with them. What a joy it is to be back together, even though I missed many stages of their lives.

I have always been guided by my faith, in which it is a most serious sin to let yourself die. Our lives and fates do not belong to us. My life is the Lord's; I know that, and if I am alive and free today, not only do I owe my life to him, but it is also not a coincidence. God entrusted me with a mission. My story will not have been without purpose because it will help other people like me. And who knows, it may even save them from a death sentence.

Those long years of imprisonment have weakened me considerably, and even if I don't have much longer to live, then

I wish to acknowledge those who defended me, for they were good men. I was surprised by Governor Salman Taseer's support because he was powerful and a Muslim. Imagine the governor of Punjab taking an interest in a girl like me—and a Christian to boot! I struggled to believe it. He warmed my heart when he came to see me in prison. It was a few weeks after the court announced my first death sentence. That morning, like every morning, I had awoken to the sounds of the chanting *muezzin*[10] coming out of the prison's loudspeakers: "*Allah Akbar, Allah Akbar!*"

I very much enjoyed hearing the prayer which, in the frozen peace of the early dawn, gave rhythm to my days. The *muezzin*'s chanting moved me because I used it as a time to pray as well, thinking of my own God. Every time I awoke, I would silently say this prayer to Jesus, confiding in him what I desired most: *Lord Jesus, I welcome your real and miraculous presence in all that I am, and this includes my wounds and frailties. I also receive you in all of my worries and all of my problems today. I am your cherished child despite all my flaws. This morning, I am opening the door to my entire being to you and rejoice in knowing that you are within me.*

I was kneeling on the humid floor of my cell, with my hands joined on my lap, when Khalil opened the door with a bang. I envied the clean, thick blanket he was wrapped in.

"Move it! We're going!"

I was worried because it was not a visitation day. At that

---

10 A man who calls Muslims to prayer from the minaret of a mosque.

time, Ashiq was only allowed to visit me once a week, and he had come to see me the night before. Ashiq, of course, lived in hiding and would frequently move, but he never stopped paying me visits despite the risks.

In the long corridor, following Khalil's footsteps, I was as feverish as someone walking to her death. The soles of his boots made his footsteps echo. I knew their sound by heart and could make out his calm, proud steps amidst thousands of others. I stared at the faded, yellowish paint peeling off the wall when, passing in front of a door, I heard a voice say, "This is your time, Asia. You're going to croak."

Other cackling voices shouted, "The noose, the noose!"

"Shut up!" Khalil stormed.

He turned left. I looked around in fear because I didn't know this hallway or its clean floor. Then, from afar, I heard a guard respectfully salute the arrival of a man. Khalil pushed open a door, and a man who looked sure of himself came toward me.

"Hello, Asia. My name is Salman Taseer. I am the governor of the Punjab, and I know your story."

He was a tall, enormous man, and behind his glasses I could already see his kindness. He sat down in a chair and asked if I was holding up alright. I remember looking at Khalil, who stood by the door. Khalil knew that Taseer was one of the most important men in Pakistan, and it was funny to watch him lower his eyes, like a boy who was caught misbehaving, dreading my response. Maybe I should have told Taseer that Khalil was mistreating me. The mighty governor could order to change my guard; he had the power to do so, but I didn't dare. Everything was already so complicated and confusing.

I whispered a shy yes before realizing I didn't look presentable. My hands were dirty, and my toenails were halfway off. My formerly orange uniform was stiff from grime, and my hair, which I hadn't washed in weeks, was covered in dirt. I felt ashamed to show myself like this. It was inappropriate.

"You'll see, Asia. We'll get you out of here," Taseer said.

His words resonated within me as a sign of deliverance. A renewed hope revived my eyes, but I gave him a sharp and piercing look: "Does that mean that I am going to be able to see my daughters again?"

"Yes, of course. I am doing everything I can to revoke your death sentence, and a lot of people support you. My friend, the Minister of Minorities, Shahbaz Bhatti, is also doing everything he can within the government. He has asked for the help of a French journalist, who has agreed to talk about it in her newspapers. But to start with, I am going to have a press conference set up here, so you can tell the whole world that you are innocent."

I didn't know what a press conference was, but I didn't dare ask him.

Before he left, he added, "You know, Asia, ever since the pope spoke out on your behalf, the whole affair has taken a bad turn. Muslims don't like Christians getting involved in our affairs. The situation is now highly critical because, in the radicals' minds, the Catholic Church has infringed upon Islam. They are going to use you, Asia, to obtain redress. But don't worry, we won't let them push you around."

A few days later, the governor kept his promise, and I came to learn what a press conference was. Earlier in the day, Khalil threw at my face the sari I had worn on the day of my incarceration.

"Get dressed. It's your time," he said, leaving just as sharply.

I didn't know what to think. If I was taking off my prisoner's uniform, then maybe I was getting out of the hellish place. Or maybe the authorities thought I would be a bit less distraught if I were hanged while wearing my own clothes. Finally rid of that uniform, I no longer felt like a prisoner. I almost felt light and confident, especially since I liked my chocolate-colored sari, which I had bought with the earnings from a harvest. Ashiq liked it, too, and said it looked good on me. From the confines of my miserable cell, I recovered a bit of dignity.

Khalil fetched me, saying nothing. For once, no insults, no mockery. He contented himself with doing his work, which, that day, involved taking me to an unfamiliar room. We entered, and the dazzling light hurt my eyes, which were used to only darkness. A lot of people and noise filled the room. My confidence was gone, and I felt like a hunted animal, threatened by the spotlights and crackling flashes. Through this hubbub of microphones and cameras, journalists looked at me as if I were a curious creature. On a stage was a table with two microphones, two empty chairs, and a small Pakistani flag.

A young, unveiled woman approached me and whispered, "Put your veil on properly, Asia. People mustn't see your hair. You don't want to provoke the bearded ones." I later learned that this woman was Shehrbano Taseer, one of the governor's daughters, who would eventually flee Pakistan following her father's death in 2011.

The governor took the stage and looked at his daughter, indicating to her that it was time. Shehrbano gently adjusted my veil and then delicately laid her hand on my shoulder to give me confidence. "Go on," the young woman with shiny, well-combed hair said. "Go ahead, Asia. Don't be afraid. Everything is going to be fine."

Only my eyes were visible beneath my full veil. I was intimidated by all of the cameras aimed at me. This was my first time speaking in front of a group of people. I sat back a bit. The governor spoke with confidence: "I have gathered you here to defend this woman, who has been unjustly sentenced to death for committing blasphemy. We can no longer turn a blind eye to the concerning rise of Islamists within our country. Is it necessary to remind people that the freedom to practice one's religion is written into our constitution? We are the heirs to our country's founder, Ali Jinnah, whose photograph watches over our offices, your houses, our schools. Jinnah set up this country in 1947 and wrote that into the constitution."

The governor removed his glasses in order to read, and I thought to myself that people usually did the reverse. But then again, I was illiterate and ultimately knew nothing of it.

"You are free," he said. "You are free to visit your mosques, your temples, and any other place of worship in the State of Pakistan. You can belong to any religion, caste, or faith. It is none of the state's business."

He lifted his head, slid his glasses back on, and continued: "That is what the founding father of our country declared in front of the first assembly of the country on August 11, 1947. For only a few years now, I have noticed that this law has become a weapon to settle or put an end to disputes. For twenty-five years, thousands of men and women have been accused of blasphemy, and all have been sentenced to a social death, if not outright death. In Sanghar, a small town five hours away from Karachi, Ghulam Rasool, a Shiite man, still mourns his young brother, Anis Mallah. A member of a caste of fishermen, Anis stood up to a rival tribe that wanted to take control of his fishing areas on a lake that teemed with fish. One day, Anis lost control of his motorbike and accidentally tripped over a monument dedicated to the Prophet Muhammad. His enemies accused him of blasphemy, and he was thrown into prison. A few months later, he was found dead in his cell. Someone had taken a brick to his head."

After a flurry of conversation, the governor turned to me and said, "Go ahead, Asia, tell them what happened." I was scared to launch into it, but Salman Taseer gave me a kind, encouraging look. Everyone in the room fell silent.

I inhaled deeply and started. "I did nothing wrong. I respect Islam, but women attacked me because I drank out of the same well as them. I am a Christian, but I love my Muslim country, and now the courts want to kill me even though I am innocent. After the women attacked me, I was beaten by a violent crowd, and the police threw me into jail. The Nankana Sahib court judge sentenced me to death, but I am innocent."

I didn't speak loudly enough for the TV cameras, but everybody listened attentively. The journalists hung on to my every word. I was uncomfortable, but this was my chance to let the world know I was innocent.

"This isn't just about Christians," the governor added. "Remember the Muslim man who was thrown into jail and murdered by his guards before he was even tried? That man didn't want to sell his land. In order to get rid of him, the man who wanted to buy it tore up pages from the Quran and left them on the other man's doorstep. This blasphemy law is unworthy of our country and our great religion. We, the heirs to Ali Jinnah, are betraying our master by flouting the principles on which he founded our country." Taseer grabbed the small Pakistani flag that was on the table and brandished it like a club before the journalists. "Green for Islam, and white for minorities."

That day, I learned that the white part of our flag was for us. It moved me to think that there was a time when minorities were well regarded in my country. We Christians had a legitimate right to live in the Islamic Republic of Pakistan.

The governor finished his appeal: "Giving this farm worker the death penalty is a cruel and inhumane sentence. I demand this woman be pardoned."

In the moment, I felt relieved to be able to tell the truth and to have the support of Governor Salman Taseer. I did not know that two months later, this press conference would cost the good governor his life. After taking his bold stance, the governor wound up in the Islamists' crosshairs. The loudspeakers of some mosques called for the murder of the "blasphemous" governor. The *mullahs* mobilized their troops all around the country to defend the blasphemy law on the streets because they considered it divine. Still, no one in Pakistan expected a figure as important as the "Great Salman" would be brutally assassinated. Minister Bhatti was the one who delivered the news to me during one of his visits to the prison.

Sitting on my *charpai*, I watched a big black fly hover around my dirty rice dish. Then the fly bolted with the speed of an arrow. I jumped when my eyes landed on Khalil, wrapped up in his warm blanket, watching me from inside my own cell. I remained speechless. How did he slip into my cell without my realizing it?

"Ha! Got you, didn't I? Come on, follow me!"

He shouted at me for not getting up, so I quickly followed him out of my cell. For the first time since I had arrived in prison,

Khalil took me to the warden's office. It was the only time that I set foot in there.

The warden was fussing over Shahbaz Bhatti, the Federal Minister for Minorities Affairs. "As head of this penitentiary," the warden gushed, "it is an honor, Mr. Minister, to welcome you here. Our inmates are very well treated, and we ask our guards to treat these women in a humane fashion. Isn't that right, Khalil?"

"Yes, Mr. Warden, sir."

I could tell Minister Bhatti, who had already visited me several times, wasn't in the best of moods. He sharply told the warden to leave us alone.

Visibly upset by the minister's response, the warden grumbled, "Of course, Mr. Minster," before vanishing with Khalil.

Shahbaz sat down in a chair and invited me to do the same. He looked concerned and said, "I have come to announce some very sad news. The governor of Punjab has been assassinated by his own bodyguard. His murderer has admitted to killing the governor for endangering Islam by taking your defense and wanting to abolish the blasphemy law."

I fell apart. How could the governor, that oh-so-powerful man, who had so much respect, have died because of me? I never imagined that the same fate would soon befall the kind minister.

"Asia, your case has become an affair of the state now. It is a highly sensitive situation, and the government doesn't want to get involved in your affair or change the law," he said, looking defeated. "But I have hired a lawyer who is going to appeal your sentence. That means that you are going to be tried again by the High Court of Justice in Lahore, which is good news."

"When?"

"We don't know. It could take some time, and that is why I have made a decision. I have asked that you be moved into an isolated cell where you will be filmed by surveillance cameras twenty-four hours a day. Your food will be brought to you raw, and you will cook it yourself in your cell. You won't go out for exercise anymore. It's going to be tough, Asia, but it is the only way to ensure your safety."

Just then, the minister's cell phone let out a beep. He read a text message then looked back up at me. "You aren't alone, Asia. I am here, and there is a Western journalist who wants to write a book about you. She has just told me so. That is our only chance, you know, for the international community to be moved by your fate."

I nodded to make it clear that I understood. Trying to keep my voice steady, I said, "I don't have any news of my children and husband. I would like to see them. I am gravely worried."

"They have all been under my protection since the beginning. They are living in hiding in a house in Lahore, and for the time being, they cannot come without risking being killed. But soon, they will visit."

I began to sob. The mustached man put his hand on my head and whispered to me, "Don't lose hope, Asia. You will be freed. I am sure of it." He was right. But I didn't know that it would take almost ten years for me to be declared innocent and freed. I don't think I would have had the courage to endure prison if I had known, then, that this was only the beginning of my ordeal.

Five days after the governor was assassinated, the minister's orders were heard. Khalil stormed into my cell like a fury: "Get up! Your Christian friend has laid down some new rules. You are going to change cells, and you're going to be far from the others. But don't rejoice, because exercise is over for you! You will never poke your nose out again. You will only breathe your own, putrid air, and that will be for your own safety allegedly. But if I were you, I would be careful."

Terrified, I didn't say anything. He doubled down, as if nothing could stop him: "Everyone wants you to die, so if you think this little move is going to save your life, then you are kidding yourself. You'll never make it out of this. Look at Salman Taseer. His own bodyguard killed him, and he became a hero across all of Pakistan. Well, I am kind of your bodyguard in this prison, if you know what I mean. And I would also like to become a national hero by getting rid of your rotten self."

I wanted to ask him why he didn't do so and what was holding him back, but I feared he would hit me.

"Listen to me closely. Even Rehman Malik, the Minister of the Interior, has said he'd kill anyone who committed blasphemy in front of him. Your Christian minister, for all that he is, has no leverage compared to him! So, you can keep making your dirty prayers if that's what makes you happy, but you won't escape from hell!"

I pray every day that the governor is resting in peace. It was only when I watched a documentary on Canadian television about my story that I understood his 2011 murder completely divided the country. The documentary described the circumstances of his death and the context surrounding it. In my cell, the only news I could get was in dribs and drabs because Ashiq wanted to protect me from events on the outside and not terrify me. He was probably right to do so. I was overwhelmed as it was without knowing very much. Khalil, for his own part, announced it to me like this: "Your guardian angel was murdered because of you. Your beloved governor, Salman Taseer, that Muslim traitor, is bathing in his own blood for defending you. Good riddance!"

Of the assassination, the television commentary said, "After eight years of good and loyal service, Mumtaz Hussain Qadri, the policeman who was Salman Taseer's bodyguard, riddled his protégé's body with twenty-nine bullets in broad daylight in Kohsar Market, an upscale market in the capital." The image was terrifying. The governor's assassin wore a broad grin on his face in front of the camera. He became a prisoner immediately, defending his act: "He deserved to be killed because he called the blasphemy law illegitimate."

The blindness of extremists is so strong. In the aftermath, I was astounded to learn that the murderer received a promotion to the rank of national hero. I saw religious people worshipping a murderer and shouting for *jihad*. At the call of the Islamists, thousands of people went out the next day to demonstrate in major cities and demand that Governor Taseer's murderer be freed. In Karachi, the Vice President of Jamaat-e-Islami called the murderer the "hero of the Ummah"[11] and warned that any sentencing would lead to new demonstrations.

People even requested that all representatives of the Vatican be thrown out of Pakistan because of the message of support for me from Pope Benedict XVI. In front of Rawalpindi, near Islamabad, the television showed hundreds of people, even lawyers, with flower necklaces awaiting the murderer's release, proclaiming him the "lion of Islam." It was scary to see such demonstrations of joy. How could anyone celebrate the actions of someone who had killed another, even in courts of justice? I was terrified. I couldn't have imagined the scale of it from my cell.

The documentary also taught me that Salman Taseer's son, Shahbaz, was not spared by the Islamists. Unsatisfied with seeing the governor assassinated, the Uzbek Taliban kidnapped Shahbaz, who was about twenty years old at the time, and forced him to endure horrible torture. The price that Salman Taseer and his family paid was so high. Tears still come to my eyes because I feel responsible for the suffering of this family, which was deprived of two of their loved ones within just a few months: one assassinated and the other kidnapped and tortured. The family must have believed Shahbaz dead. Almost five

---

11 Community of Muslims, the Islamic Nation.

years went by before he managed to escape and return to his family. Five long years of horrible suffering! My heart breaks to think of it.

Once he was finally free, Shahbaz declined to speak to journalists, and I understand his decision. Maybe he was in too much shock. He probably wanted to resume a normal life with his family. But how can one resume a normal life after enduring so much suffering at such a young age? The documentary said that he was ultimately willing to bear witness and tell his story but only by indirectly speaking to people online, in a sort-of notebook known as Twitter, where people could read what he wrote day after day. At first, he mostly talked about his joy at seeing his wife again and didn't talk about the abuse. Little by little, though, he began to share the whole truth of his experience, which made me cry in agony.

The Islamists recorded unbearable videos of the torture they inflicted upon him and sent the videos to his family. They whipped him, lacerated his back, and covered his wounds in salt. They sewed his mouth shut, depriving him of food for days. They tore the nails out of his hands and feet and buried him alive for several days in a row. The Taliban would show him pictures of his family members, insulting them and telling him that they had forgotten him. Hearing all of those insults and threats tore his heart up, but he never doubted for a second that his loved ones were fighting to find him. He said the solitude sometimes drove him mad, but he had a best friend: a spider he named Peter! Sort of like me and my little rat, which I named little rat. His guards moved him around from one place to another to keep rescuers from finding him. They wanted to trade him for money and the release of imprisoned Islamists. On TV, they mentioned a ransom of two billion rupees! Who on earth could pay such a ransom?

One day, a group of Taliban members—Afghan ones, this time—captured Shahbaz and his guards. At first, the Afghan Taliban refused to believe Shahbaz was a prisoner, and they imprisoned him just like the Uzbek Taliban had. Fortunately, one of the Afghan Taliban members eventually understood that Shahbaz was not a member of the Uzbek Taliban and helped Shahbaz escape. Once freed, Shahbaz walked miles and miles despite being weak from abuse and exhaustion. He reached a village and was able to call his mother and let her know that he was alive. Shahbaz was found a few days after his father's assassin was hanged for his crime.

I think what Shahbaz Taseer endured is worse than what I went through. Still, I understand so well what he must have felt: a mixture of strength and despair in the daily struggle, hour by hour, in order to hold his head high and keep moving. When you have a good heart like Shahbaz, you find strength even in the worst situations. On Twitter, he explained how much he thought of his father during his imprisonment and how he would talk to him. Shahbaz wanted to live up to the great man his father had been, as Shahbaz also fought injustices against women and minorities. It also happens that Shahbaz is a pious man, and prayer helped him endure his horrible circumstances. It brings joy to my heart to think that he, too, was carried by his faith and by prayer. I know that God supported us both.

People are fascinated with his story and continue to read his words and support him by sending him messages and asking questions. What is amazing is that Shahbaz is able to make jokes about the ordeal. He said that what he thought had changed the most after five years was his wife's haircut! He wrote that even though his guards were cruel, "they had cool turbans!" Shahbaz is able to make light of things, but I cannot. I don't think I will ever be able to do so. I believe his humor hides his suffering and sadness, and I think that, like me, he must have nightmares and a mind often tormented by fear. One cannot remain the same after having been through hell on earth.

I pray to God every day for Shahbaz Taseer and his family. Thanks to people like him, I will never stop loving my country and having faith for its future. That man's courage is incredible. He continues to communicate with people on his internet journal. He shares his tastes, his new joys, and everything he wants to do again to feel alive, like eat pizza and watch soccer. Shahbaz knows his former guards sometimes read his journal. To talk about it with humor is a way for him to show the extremists that they failed to break him. Instead, he is even stronger, full of love for his country, and will never stop fighting against injustice.

Using images from the time, the Canadian documentary explained how, out of cowardice and fear of reprisal, all of the members of the government promised to never reform the anti-blasphemy laws—all but the Minister of Minorities, Shahbaz Bhatti. The good minister, who was the only Christian in the government, still had the boldness to campaign for me despite his own father suffering a heart attack on the same day of Governor Salman Taseer's assassination. Bhatti's father knew his son would be next on the extremists' list, and how terribly correct he had been.

Two months after Governor Taseer's assassination, Bhatti was slain in central Islamabad. He was in a car and on his way to visit his mother. The Pakistani Taliban claimed the assassination and left leaflets at the scene of the crime. The Vatican agreed to inquire into the matter of his death, and various churches across Pakistan have since gathered requests for his beatification. Every day, I pray the church will officially recognize that he sacrificed his own life to save the lives of others.

In the three months following the deaths of my protectors, I gave myself over to grief and shame for having caused so much suffering to those who supported my innocence. I still feel tremendous sadness but also pride and joy. It means there is still hope for a better future and that one must never stop praying or believing in it.

By March of 2011, Anne-Isabelle was the only person going out of her way to see me in prison. Despite her obstinacy and the deaths of the minister and governor, the authorities certainly did not want a journalist (and foreigner) visiting me or writing a book about my story. She and Ashiq came up with a plan to make my voice heard outside the walls of that prison. She would ask Ashiq questions through her personal translator, and he would then ask them to me. She wanted to know, in detail, what I did with my days: what time I got up, what time I went to sleep, what I ate, and the size of my cell. I was surprised she took such an interest in my miserable situation as a prisoner. I would respond, and Ashiq would verbally share my answers with Anne-Isabelle, who waited for him in a car outside of the prison.

The book gave our wounded hearts a small glimmer of hope. Ashiq would tell me that she was often hurried and impatient but also kind and charitable. Anne-Isabelle had also asked Ashiq about our personal life, as well as the lives of our daughters. Then, as summer neared, Ashiq came to see me with Tahir, my first lawyer who spoke English, to translate the book Anne-Isabelle had written for me. When he finished reading, I couldn't get over it. It was my life, my thoughts, my torments. She had told it all as if she had been there with me inside my cell.

"This book is going to be translated around the whole world. Asia, you're going to be as famous as the pope!" Ashiq crooned.

I opened my eyes wide and thought back to what Minister Shahbaz Bhatti had said to me. "Ashiq," I started, "Shahbaz Bhatti told me this would be the only way for me to get out of here. According to him, the whole world would need to know my story in order for me to be better defended."

Back then, neither Ashiq nor I understood how a book

would help to get me out of prison. But when the book became available for purchase in bookstores, I saw the difference it made. My family was invited to France, Spain, Switzerland, and Italy to talk about my story. The book touched the hearts of people, and because of that, Anne-Isabelle was able to call on political figures and even talk about me to the United Nations— in front of delegates from around the world.

After my transfer into solitary confinement, I no longer had access to the visiting room. From behind my cell gates, I could barely see Ashiq's face. One day, though, I could see that his face was crumpled.

"What's going on, Ashiq? You're making me worry. It's not our girls, is it?"

"No, no, everything is fine with them," he said. "Don't worry. It's just that yesterday, when Anne-Isabelle came to see us and bring the manuscript, she made a terrible announcement. She is leaving for France the day after tomorrow because she, too, is receiving death threats in Pakistan. The French secret services sent her a warning. She's been receiving anonymous phone calls, and the caller tells her she's going to be murdered for writing a book against Islam with Asia." Ashiq then told me about the rest of their conversations with Anne-Isabelle.

"But that isn't true," our daughter Eisham had protested to Anne-Isabelle. "You are writing a book about Mom."

"Of course," Anne-Isabelle had said. "But you know very well that you can't reason with extremists. And even though I am sorry that I can't stay here anymore, I put my life and those of my children in jeopardy."

"Oh, but I didn't know you had children! How old are they? Do you have pictures?"

"Yes, Eisham, I'll show you them. But first, listen to me, because this is important. I will continue to support you from Paris, and thanks to this book, you won't have any money problems, because you will be getting what we call royalties."

Eisham was touched and responded, "You are our only chance now. You mustn't forget us once you are back in your country."

The news of Anne-Isabelle's departure was devastating. Eisham was right; at the time, Anne-Isabelle was the last person supporting us in Pakistan. I feared she would abandon us. We would be out of sight and out of mind. And I would have completely understood; our country is so different for Westerners. Besides, how could she help me from France? It was too far, and her life would be full of other things.

"I think she'll forget us, Ashiq, which is to be expected. Plus, she is a journalist. She will move on to tell other peoples' stories."

Ashiq assured me that she would still be there for me, but his expression was not convincing. The future would show me that I was wrong. She managed to get me out of prison and has always been present in our lives. Today, she continues to care about our well-being, even though we have already been saved. She became a member of our family.

Chapter 8

MULTAN PRISON

Malice, to make itself even worse,
dons the mask of goodness.
PUBLILIUS SYRUS, *MORAL SAYINGS*

Another two years went by in prison. The days followed one another and were cruelly, tirelessly alike. Khalil continued to abuse me, and I continued to wait, frozen with anxiety. Visits from my family were like rare breaths of fresh air, but they had found a rhythm without me. My loved ones needed to laugh sometimes and experience joy, which felt both painful and reassuring.

Ashiq introduced me to a new friend of his: Joseph, a schoolmaster at a small establishment in Lahore. After Anne-Isabelle left for France, he, too, was moved by my fate, and he took my daughters under his wing. But I would learn much later that this man, whom I initially thought to be good, was worse than evil. At first, Joseph helped us. He could read and write in English, and he owned a computer, which allowed us to stay in touch with Anne-Isabelle, who kept her promise to stay in touch and support us. Joseph also found Ashiq a small job to help him earn a few rupees. Ashiq watched schoolchildren during recess and lined them up at the end of classes.

In December of 2012, my daughters, who I had only seen once in four years, surprised me in the loveliest way. They visited me on Christmas and brought a cake! It was my nicest gift. In my language, to say Christmas, you say "*vada din,*" which means "great day," and it was a great day. When I saw them arrive, I trembled. I was so touched and happy to see them, but I was also worried and scared that they might think I had changed or was different. I feared they wouldn't recognize their mom, but no! My girls jumped and cried with joy. They looked at me the same way they always had. My only regret was that I couldn't touch them. We were separated by bars.

Joseph had also come with Ashiq and my daughters, and he found the situation unacceptable, so he went to find the warden. When he returned, Joseph said, "He has agreed to let you out of your cell, Asia, and to provide us with a small room just for us."

I was so happy! I hugged my darling children all afternoon long. Eisha, who is a bit challenged, seemed calm and had fewer tics than usual; as for my little Eisham, she told me she wanted to remain by my side even though she was afraid of the dark. Together, we cut the cake into generous pieces and experienced conflicting emotions: outbursts of laughter mixed in with tears that we tried to hold back. Christmas is truly a special holiday that brings back memories and reminds us of our hopes.

Back in my cell alone, I thanked aloud all of the people around the world who had shown compassion for me, as if they could hear me: "My God, I was so happy to be able to celebrate the birth of our Lord with my husband and children. I would have liked to be free for Christmas, but I trust in God's plan, and maybe that will happen next year. I want to express my gratitude for all of the faithful people who pray for me and fight for my freedom. It is thanks to the strength that your prayers give me that I am still alive."

At the time, I had hoped it would be my last Christmas in prison, but I went on to spend another five locked away, and not all would be as festive. Despite the appeals submitted by my lawyers and the international momentum gained by Anne-Isabelle, my legal situation remained at a standstill. I was waiting for the High Court of Lahore to try me again, but my trial date kept getting pushed back.

The days in prison were punctuated by little nothings that you invent if you have some imagination. I would picture myself as a simple tourist who was simply passing through, or I would imagine that each day in prison was my last before being freed. Then, in June 2013, a significant event occurred in my drab, monotonous prisoner's life. I found out that I would be changing prisons. When Khalil told me about it with a hint of disappointment, I should have felt relief at not having to deal with him anymore, but change is naturally scary: you know what you are leaving behind, but you have no idea whether you are heading into something better or worse.

The most terrible thing about my move was that my new placement in Multan was more than a ten-hour drive from Lahore—a long and expensive journey for my family to make. When Ashiq and Joseph came to see me for the first time in my new prison and realized how dangerous and expensive it would be for them to visit, they alerted Anne-Isabelle and sent a letter to the attorney general, begging him to keep me close to my family. After four long years spent in Sheikhupura prison with Khalil as my appointed guard, I thought my new life as a prisoner in Multan couldn't be worse. I was wrong.

I was transferred in the night. When I arrived at dawn, the guards told me to undress and put on a white uniform, which I assumed wouldn't stay white for long. The woman who would have eventually become my executioner accompanied me to my cell, which was a little bit bigger than the previous one and had a little window with fitted grills. After giving the room a quick scan, I noticed that the bed was lopsided and that one of the legs was broken.

I humbly asked the guard if we could change it, but she didn't answer me. She wasn't chatty, but at least she didn't terrorize me like Khalil, who derived so much joy from shouting at me. Her round face and even features made me think she must have been pretty, but she never allowed emotion to show on her face. When the door closed behind me, I lay down on the wobbly bed with my eyes wide open. The endless journey in the police car had worn me out.

The sound of keys clicking in the lock pulled me out of my reverie. I did not know whether I had slept or, if I had, for how long. When you have been locked up for that many years, time becomes blurry, and you lose all points of reference. The noises in my new prison were foreign to me: keys jangling on a chain, doors opening and closing, guards' footsteps. My guard entered and brought a bucket full of clear water. The sound of her mules sliding around the floor was a change from Khalil's stomping boots. She lifted her head my way without looking me in the eye and said, "This is for you to wash with. Your meal will come later."

Her voice was warm and reassuring. Feeling confident, I introduced myself. "I'm Asia. What should I call you?" She set the bucket down without answering and then left the room slowly, with the same sliding steps with which she had entered.

My guard later told me her name was Kadeeja, and each following day, I thanked God for sending me this angel and recited the prayer my grandmother had taught me when I was a little girl: *Father, thank you for protecting us through the night. Thank you for this new day and the health you have given us. Lord, remain with us while we work, eat, and play. Fill us with your love and that of those around us. Amen.*

My grandmother had me repeat that prayer throughout the day, so I never forgot it. She was like a second mother to me.

I even called her *Amii*, which is what I called my mother. I never knew my grandfather. He died fighting in the war against India. Amii spoke of him to me frequently. She would tell me that her husband had been an honest, kind man and that I should marry someone like him, which I did! Amii, my parents, my brothers, my sisters, and I all lived under the same roof in a humble house in Kutupura, which is ten kilometers away from Ittan-Walli.

My heart aches at the idea of never again seeing the village I grew up in, even if it was a very humble one. The village was lost amongst the sugar cane fields and not mentioned on any road signs because it was not a welcoming place. The waterways functioned as an open-air sewage system and ran alongside the small houses, which were made of sundried cow dung shaped into bricks. Even for a farm girl like me, it stank. More recently, a lot of foreign journalists have visited Ittan-Walli to meet my accusers, who still live there. The most insignificant village in the world has become famous.

In my new prison in Multan, my weeks went by without news from anyone—neither my lawyer nor Ashiq. Day in and day out, I was preoccupied with uncertainty. I often asked Kadeeja if my family knew where I was, but she would shrug her shoulders and tell me she didn't know.

One morning, I felt pain in my eyes and had a terrible headache. Over the next few days, the pain got worse, and my eyes stung so badly that I couldn't keep them open. Then, in the middle of the night, a burning heat and an unquenchable thirst seemed to devour my insides. I could feel the roots of my teeth moving around inside my gums, giving me the unpleasant impression that they might fall out. My stomach was so taut and bloated that it was difficult to move, and every time I needed to relieve myself in the hole in the corner of my cell, I panicked at the thought of losing my teeth. It was a greater struggle to get back to my bed. Once there, I didn't dare move out of fear of reawakening the pain.

I dragged myself along like this for several days, telling myself I had become rotten, as Khalil predicted. Feverish and delirious, I could not drink the glasses of water that Kadeeja wordlessly set on the ground. She didn't treat me, but her presence comforted and encouraged me. With the help of another guard, she replaced my wonky bed with a sturdy *charpai*. Because I was too weak to stand on my own, Kadeeja carried me. She dared to touch me, which I found reassuring because it was proof that she wasn't disgusted by a Christian woman and that she would behave kindly toward me.

In my feverish delirium, I thought of my beloved mother. She worked hard in the sugarcane fields. She was brave, my mother, and she never rested—except when we would cuddle up together at night. She fell very ill one day and, like me, began to sweat, shiver, and speak incoherently. I was about ten years old because I had to wear my *dupatta*[12] out of respect whenever the *muezzin* issued the call to prayer. I was doing the laundry,

---

12 Veil.

caring for the goats, and tending the small vegetable garden. She no longer had the strength to drink, so I would lift the cup to her mouth and wipe her forehead with a wet cloth. I stayed near her for as long as possible because I was terrified of losing her forever in my absence.

I spoke to her in my fever. *Mom, I feel like my heart is escaping, flying off like a little bird. My blood is burned up from the moaning. Come back to my side. I am lost. I need you to fight all of this. I am tired, sick, worn out, and exhausted, but I will continue to fight for my wonderful family.*

Between bouts of burning delirium, I felt an invisible presence next to me, and I knew deep down that it was connected to my family. I would have liked so much to have been able to write to my husband and children. If I hadn't been completely exhausted, I could have at least dictated a letter to Kadeeja. I believed I was living my final hours, and I thought about how I had messed everything up. I hoped my family would be understanding toward me and not resent me too much for abandoning them. *My God, give me courage,* I prayed. *I need it so. I trust in you and offer you my all.* For the lack of something better and in a burst of energy, I wrote to them in my thoughts, knowing they would never hear it.

My gentle Ashiq, my darling children,

I love you. From the depths of my cell, you are all I have thought about over the years. And you've allowed me to hold on for all this time because you were my strength, which helped me carry a little bit of joy in my heart ever since that dreadful judgment. Life has spoiled me so much by giving you to me. I was sure that we would be reunited one day and celebrate my return together. I have dreamt of our reunion every night.

But the years I spent in prison have weakened me considerably, and I have been grievously ill for a few days. I think I will die soon. Despite my best, I will not be able to overcome this new challenge. I am not being treated, and nobody cares about me here. If it weren't for the rage of these men to see me disappear, I would be hugging you and taking care of you. I would have liked to see you grow up and to grow old by your sides.

I am asking you to be brave. This is a difficult ordeal for all of us, and you didn't deserve this. It must be difficult to understand the injustice that has befallen me. I cried when I was sentenced to death. The *mullahs* have not relinquished the pressure they put on the judges, who lack courage. I ask you to have that courage instead. I am not afraid. Everything will be fine, and in the name of other convicts like me, being courageous is sort of like being encouraging!

You know that I am innocent. The accusations

against me are lies. I am stubborn. I may have committed the sin of pride, but I am not evil or violent. The judges decided to believe the slander of those mean women, out of fear of the *mullahs.* They sent me to my death in a matter of minutes. An unjust and cruel death. If this illness does not kill me, then I shall be hanged. I think of Jesus' suffering on the cross, and I want to be brave like him. I pray for my soul's salvation and for yours too.

My Ashiq, thank you for your generosity and tenderness. I thank Jesus every day for giving me such a good, brave, and loving husband. I was immensely happy with you for twenty-two years. It is a blessing to have been able to find each other and to experience a loving union when that is not the custom in our part of the world. We always got along so well. I feel guilty that I am unable to be close to you and carry out my roles as a wife and mother. I know you will take good care of our children and protect them.

My tall Imran, who I raised like my own son, I wish you a happy life and a good wife. Be as loving as your father was to me. My lovely Nassima, I leave this world joyfully knowing that you will soon be wed and warmly welcomed into your fiancé's family. I would have liked to know my grandchildren.

Give your father that joy and raise your children with Christian charity—the way we did. My tender Eisha, you are still a very young girl, even if you are fifteen years old. The Lord has chosen you. He wanted you to forever remain an innocent soul because you were born with challenges. You are a gift to your father and me. You have always been smiling and loving. You cannot understand why your mother was taken away from you. I know it is you, my sweet Sidra, at seventeen years, who tenderly cares for your sister and the upkeep of the house. That isn't what I wanted for you. I blame myself for making you grow up too fast. And you, my very small Eisham, you will grow up without your mother when you are only thirteen. It's unfair. Your father promised me you would continue to go to school. That makes me proud. You will be educated. You will be able to read and write, and you will be able to fight injustice. I wish you a lovely life.

Don't be sad, my children. Pray to God every day. He is your Father in heaven, and I am entrusting you into his hands. I will always be with you. I will protect you. Draw strength from this trial and do nothing foolish against the rules in this country nor against Muslims.

Here in jail, the other women's stories have

taught me that you were lucky to have a family full of love and parents who love each other and who are respectful and brave. We wanted our family to be warm like the sun, even if we have no material possessions. Your father and I have worked to raise you with Christian charity by placing the values of our faith at the center of what we passed on to you. That is our greatest wealth. I am leaving with my heart at peace because you are kind and generous. You will be honest people. This last goodbye is painful for me and costs my heart dearly, but celebrate in your own hearts, because I will soon be in the arms of the Lord.

My beloved children and Ashiq: my loving heart of a wife and mother will stay with you forever. Farewell, my children. I hug you closely in my heart and send you tender kisses. I love you.

—Mom

Then, one day, for no apparent reason, the fever suddenly stopped, and my head started to hurt less. I was surprised at my own toughness and told myself that God must not have wanted me to die in this fashion.

The prison in Multan had no surveillance cameras, and my food was brought to me already cooked. I wondered if someone had poisoned me, like Bouguina had been. When Kadeeja slipped into my cell, she didn't seem surprised to see that I was doing better. I thanked her for not abandoning me.

"I was just doing my job," she said.

"No," I insisted. "Feeling your presence helped me pull through."

"If you like, you can go to the TV room. You are allowed."

I celebrated this news under my breath without knowing the troubles that it would cause me.

"Thank you. I still feel weak, but yes, I would like to do that soon."

In our little house in Ittan-Walli, we were able to buy a slightly dented TV set, which we hid inside a closet in case the Taliban came. For them, TV was a sin because women looked at men, and men looked at women. Ashiq, the children, and I liked watching an Indian program called *Tara*. It was broadcast every day and followed the adventures of Tara and her four friends, who had stormy relationships with their mothers-in-law, who were attached to the old traditions. It also talked about love.

Once I perked up again, Kadeeja took me, as promised, to the TV room and left right away. Nobody else was in the room, and I figured the other inmates must be praying, or perhaps they didn't want the Christian woman to mix with the Muslim women. The on-screen images showed an old, bearded man zealously reading verses from the Quran. I pushed the button to change the channel, hoping for a bit of entertainment. What a joy it was to see that *Tara* was on! I pulled my chair up closer. I felt like I had been magically transported to my previous life.

A few minutes later, an inmate came in quietly. I moved aside a bit so that she could see the screen, too, but she didn't show any sign of thanks or interest in the program. Two other women came in, whispering to each other, and they stayed at the back of the room. This was the first time that I had been face-to-face with other inmates, and I was beginning to feel uncomfortable. When a lot of women came in, one of them bellowed out to me: "Who said you could change the program?"

"Sorry, I didn't know. No one told me anything, and I was alone. But you...You can change it if you want."

The enraged woman marched over to me and slapped me. Then she shouted, "Because of you, we're going to be beaten with sticks. Your program is abject and dishonorable!"

I rolled into a ball on the ground, covering my face with my arm. Women struck me multiple times, and then an authoritative voice rang out, rising above the others: "That's enough!"

I recognized Kadeeja's voice instantly, although I never heard her raise her voice before. She grabbed me by the arm to help me stand up, and I was touched. My guardian angel then accompanied me back to my cell without saying a word. Still in shock, I failed to thank her and regretted it.

In my squalid dungeon, with a lump in my throat, I asked God why he was so mad at me. Was my fate to be slapped around my whole life? I thought TV might bring me a bit of respite, a breath of fresh air. I honestly didn't think I was doing anything bad, and I certainly did not wish to offend anyone whatsoever. I realized I would never go back to the TV room with the other inmates. I assumed the ordeal was behind me—unaware of the consequences that *Tara* would have within the prison itself.

The following night, someone slipped into my cell, punched me, and beat me with a stick. The person left as quickly as they had come, leaving me in shock. I didn't dare say anything to Kadeeja when she brought me my food dish. I didn't want to cause any more trouble. I just had to hold on until the courts reviewed my case again. The night after that, I awakened once again to blows to my head, stomach, and ribs. I didn't know who my persecutor was, but they wielded a stick better than anyone. I howled in pain, but I was still alive. In poor condition but alive. Despite the TV ordeal, Kadeeja remained as silent, still, and expressionless as before.

Day after day, I felt weaker. I hurt all over. Sometimes, when it was very hot, my skin felt as if it were melting off my bones, and I struggled to breathe. When I searched for air, my lungs burned. Enduring prison became increasingly difficult. To stay strong, I would think of Ashiq and the children, but it was hard. I was cramped inside my cell and could no longer stand the stench. In my house, things were always clean. I was careful to have a well-kept house so that it would be welcoming. In prison, that was impossible. The water coming out of the pipe was so black that I wondered how it could possibly wash anybody. My skin itched and burned. Pimples and red blotches covered my face and sometimes bled. I looked like a beggar.

The women in the TV room treated me cruelly, and one of them said that I was poisoning the air and that the infestation of fleas and lice was my fault. All because I was nothing but "a dirty impure Christian." It was unfair and untrue, and I finally worked up the courage to tell Kadeeja about my nights of horror: "I have to tell you that sometimes at night, someone comes into my cell and beats me in my sleep without saying anything."

"You must have done something bad," she answered flatly.

Her emotionless tone surprised me. I realized she must know something and didn't want to tell me, so as not to attract trouble. I was slowly losing trust in the person who, until then, I considered my only ally in prison. I suddenly felt lost and deeply alone. But that night, I decided to stay awake and face whoever was hurting me.

I sat on my bed, pulled my knees to my chest, and waited. That was the only position my body could be in that kept me from falling asleep. I had no idea what time it was, and no sounds had come from the hallway for a long time. I was determined to unmask whoever was coming into my cell and beating me, but keeping my eyelids open became more and more of a challenge. I thought back to Kadeeja, who hadn't seemed surprised by what I had told her, and the more I thought about it, the more I wondered if she was complicit with it. To relax my numb muscles and to stay focused on my persecutor's imminent arrival, I changed positions. More time went by, and I started to feel dizzy with tiredness. My head swayed back and forth.

I heard the *muezzin*'s singing, which drew me out of semi-consciousness. That meant it was five in the morning, and I had fallen asleep without realizing it. Why had no one come to beat me that night? I noticed that Kadeeja had dropped off my water pot, and the tea inside was still steaming. To catch up on sleep and to be sure that I stayed awake at all costs that night, I slept for part of the day without seeing or speaking to her. I eventually stopped sleeping at night altogether from having forced myself to stay awake so many nights.

Then, one night, the beam of a flashlight crossed the threshold of my door. My heart stopped beating. I held my breath. Hunched over in my bed, I heard the door open softly. My persecutor had slipped inside my cell. I immediately recognized the sliding footsteps. It was Kadeeja! An enormous sense of relief washed over me.

"Kadeeja, I was so scared. Thank you for coming to see if I was alright. Can you stay for a bit, so I can doze off for a few minutes?"

She turned off her flashlight, no doubt so as not to be noticed, and dealt a forceful blow to my heel.

"What on earth are you doing?" I exclaimed. The pain spread throughout my entire body. Tears welled in my eyes. "Stop it, please! Stop it, Kadeeja! You're going to break all of my limbs! Why are you doing this to me?"

Without any regard for my distress, she continued hitting me, breathing ever so loudly. Drops of her sweat fell on my face. I was witnessing and experiencing an explosion of hatred.

"Please, I beg you...Who are you?"

Only our panting broke the silence. Kadeeja let go of her stick and violently grabbed me by the hair. She gasped and then threw me in a fury.

"I trusted you," she finally said. "I treated you like a human being and got in trouble because of you. The warden summoned me after you put your evil program on the TV. I have seven mouths to feed myself, while you are lost forever." Before leaving, she added, "You had better be quiet about this, or I'll hit you even harder."

My limbs shook. I was in shock. Exhausted and broken, I eventually fell asleep, but I understood that my guardian angel had become the angel of death.

The following morning, Kadeeja brought me my bucket of water and my bowl, but we neither spoke nor exchanged glances. During the day, I was alone with my shame, cloistered in my cell, and at night, I was alone with death, waiting for my executioner to beat me. Ten days or so passed, and I felt doubly imprisoned. I was deprived of freedom and unable to speak to anyone. And then, as Kadeeja brought me a glass of water, she finally opened her mouth: "You have visitors."

Stunned, I stood up immediately and limped to the visiting room. It was Ashiq and Joseph! Kadeeja left us alone. The tears I had been holding back let loose. I had so many questions to ask, but I had a lump in my throat.

Ashiq's face fell when he saw me. "You don't look so good, Asia. You're limping, and you have black circles under your eyes."

I sobbed even harder, unable to speak.

"We're sorry it took so long to visit you," Ashiq whispered. "We tried to come a month ago, but we had an accident. The Islamists put a car in the middle of the road, and we wound up in a ditch. My heel was injured, but the paramedics arrived right away and bandaged it."

"I was miraculously unhurt!" Joseph exclaimed.

"But afterward," Ashiq continued, "we had to gather funds to buy a new car, and we had to move because the Islamists spotted us. They were lurking near our house."

"And now, are you safe?" I asked.

"Yes, I'm fine. But what about you? How is it here? Is it better than the other prison?"

"The woman who brought me in here beats me every night. There was an issue with the other inmates in the TV room, and she's been hitting me ever since."

Ashiq put his head in his hands. Joseph was so shocked that he abruptly rose from his chair.

"I fell very ill too," I continued. "I don't think I am going to make it here."

"We aren't going to let this happen, Asia," Ashiq promised. "I'm going to talk to the warden and then to the journalist. People need to know what is going on."

But the warden told Ashiq that if he leaked the story, Ashiq would never be allowed to visit me again. Ashiq and Joseph left totally defeated. Fortunately, someone made an anonymous call from within the prison and alerted the local media, and Anne-Isabelle made such a stir abroad that the warden, under pressure from the government, was forced to fire Kadeeja. Sometimes, I dream about her. I regret having trusted her so much in the beginning. She hurt me more than Khalil did. He was awful, granted, but his intentions were always clear.

After that unfortunate episode, my conditions improved inside Multan prison. I was allowed one hour of solitary walking in the courtyard, and my food was brought to me raw. Now responsible for cooking it myself, I welcomed the task as a small distraction to my dull days. But among those changes, the most important one was that I was assigned a Christian guard, probably to avoid more problems. Her name was Mamita, and she read the Bible to me every morning. She was a great comfort and provided the affection, energy, and confidence that I needed until I left the prison in October 2018. I loved Mamita like a sister, and I miss her often. Sadly, I will never see her again.

Chapter 9

SECOND DEATH SENTENCE

Extreme justice is an extreme injustice.
TERENCE, *HEAUTON TIMORUMENOS*

The years went by, long and heavy. When they visited, Ashiq and Joseph would tell me about external developments. Well, not all the time. I learned rather late that my trials before the High Court of Lahore and then in front of the Supreme Court had been postponed again and again. I don't know how the justice system works in other countries, but in Pakistan justice is slow, as if they are unaware that we, the accused, are not waiting to be tried in the comfort of our homes but in prison. I lost almost ten years of my life just waiting, and nothing can make up for the lost time.

To spare me these disappointments, Ashiq never told me when the date of my trial was decreed. With each postponement, I spent more months and years locked up, dreaming of freedom. While waiting to go to Canada, six months after I was definitively acquitted and supposedly free to come and go, Ashiq, who was "in transit" with me, explained to me how he would find out that my trials had been postponed. In March of 2014, for instance, happy to be going to the High Court of Lahore to witness my appeal and wholeheartedly believing that I would be declared innocent, he received his first official summons and went to the trial at the stated time.

He described the day to me: "Joseph and I woke up at six thirty a.m. because we had to drive for an hour and a half to get to the courthouse. We didn't want to make a bad impression by arriving late. We were scheduled to meet with the first lawyer you had at eight, an hour before the hearing. The lawyer was confident and thought the court was ready to declare your innocence because many of what he called 'procedural errors' were made. It was looking like it was going to be a beautiful day. You had been in jail for four and a half years, and it was time for us to reunite.

"When we arrived at court, nobody spoke to us. We came across an ordinary piece of paper hanging on the door that read: 'The court is in recess today. The hearing is postponed to fifteen days from now.' We didn't understand why. The lawyer tried to find out more. He asked a ton of questions to people who did not want to answer him. Finally, a magistrate agreed to see us later that afternoon. He told us that one of the judges had stepped down. The magistrate didn't want to tell us why, but according to the lawyer, since your case was a special one, there were several possible explanations. According to him, either the judge was a Muslim, or the Islamists pressured him, or he had a family matter to attend."

The problem was that NGOs kept revealing the court date in the media, thinking they were helping, but the Islamists would also find out and then threaten the judges to convict me. Some of the NGOs continued to broadcast the date of my trial to attract foreign aid but kept the funds for themselves. In Canada, I found out that Joseph was among the people who stole from these donations. He would collect money in my name but keep all or nearly all of it for himself. Ashiq even confided in me that Joseph seemed disappointed when I was freed. I suppose he knew from that point on that he would no longer be able to gain from my suffering.

Two weeks later, the trial was postponed, and we had to wait another year of endless adjournments for my trial to finally take place. We were all confident because the Court of Lahore was, after all, much less subject to pressure from the *mullahs* than the little neighborhood court. The court didn't think it useful for me to be present at my own appeal, so I only learned the results when Ashiq and Joseph, having taken every possible precaution, came to visit me on October 16, 2014, a date that is forever carved into my memory. Their faces looked crumpled and defeated.

Ashiq was in shock, so Joseph told me the terrible news: "When the three judges opened the hearing, about twenty *mullahs* slipped into the room, which chilled the air considerably. Once the facts were established, the judge allotted very uneven speaking times to the lawyers: forty minutes for the prosecution and barely ten for your lawyer, who was interrupted by one of the judges halfway through his plea. The court systematically rejected his arguments that claimed the previous trial included perjured testimony and false accusations. The judges didn't need much time to deliberate before they declared, 'Given Article 295 C, the High Court of Lahore confirms the death sentencing of Asia Bibi for the crime of blasphemy.'"

The echo of that sentence still resonates in my head. Ashiq's face was devastated with sorrow, and I closed my eyes, wishing I could turn back time.

"When the verdict was given," Joseph continued, "a dozen *imams*, including your village *mullah*, Qari Salaam, celebrated the court's decision, saying they were going to hand out candy to their Muslim brothers and your sentence was a victory for Islam."

All traces of warmth left my body. Inside, everything was cold, dark, and sad. Even my tears quit running. Joseph told me we had thirty days to submit a final appeal to the Supreme Court and that we should pray they would accept it. If they didn't, then our last chance was to obtain a presidential pardon. My heart turned to ash after yet another disappointment.

I devoted the following days to reciting this prayer: *My God, you are the one who has determined my fate. I don't want to fight any longer, for only you know what is good for me. You chose this life for me, and I trust your plans. What will happen on the other side once everything rolls over into eternity, I don't know. All I believe is that love awaits me. Now that my time is near and the cross points to the threshold that I must step beyond, it is toward your love that I walk. It is toward your love that I extend my arms. When I die, don't cry. Love is peacefully taking hold of me. If I am afraid (and why wouldn't I be?), then remind me that love awaits. Yes, Father in heaven, I approach you like a child and entrust myself to your love.*

Multan prison only permitted visits once every two weeks, so when Ashiq and Joseph came to see me next, they were optimistic once more, whereas I no longer had faith that I would ever be free. Joseph told me that in France, Anne-Isabelle was talking about me in the newspapers and on TV. I decided I wanted to thank Anne-Isabelle for all her efforts by dictating a letter to Joseph, who would translate and send it to her:

Thursday, October 20, 2014

My dear friend and beloved sister,

I am going to die. I found out a few days ago, and you know it too. When Joseph told me the terrible news, my heart felt empty. I couldn't feel anything anymore. I was like stone, and Ashiq's eyes glazed over. I spent a long time trying to catch my breath, and my mouth was as dry as if the sun had been on it forever. I wanted to call a guard and have them execute me on the spot while I requested God's grace. Tears streamed down Ashiq's red face. I struggled to compose myself.

I begged God to free me, to let me out of this prison and go back to our old life, and stupidly, I felt reassured when he told me the children knew nothing about the judgment—as if that would change anything about our fate! I think part of me was soothed by the idea that they were delighted to see their mom soon. Then he explained to me that hope was left. First, he found a new lawyer, a Muslim, who is going to submit an appeal to the Supreme Court. And then there is you! Ashiq and Joseph tell me you have been talking about me and asking your president to ask my president to grant me a presidential pardon. But my friend, I may already be dead by the time this letter reaches you.

I am so tired of everything. I am tired from having fought for so long. I feel my heart crumbling. It shrivels away inside my chest. Now, I would like to entrust myself to God. He alone will decide whether I should be hanged from a noose. I would like you to stop wasting your time trying to save me. You must think of yourself now. You have a lovely life to live in your country. My own country is so complicated!

I would have so much liked to meet you, hug you, and look at you. You are one of my own, and when I am in heaven, you will always have a place in my heart.

—Asia

In hindsight, I realize how hopeless I felt. I truly thought I would never meet Anne-Isabelle, which goes to show that one must be patient and not lose hope. She responded a short time later with a letter that was full of hope:

Monday, November 10, 2014

My dearest Asia,

I am asking you to be brave, very brave. You aren't allowed to give up now, not after you have held on for five years of imprisonment. You must know that the whole world is ready to welcome you and that you have your place among us and with your family, who is counting on you. Lots of things are in motion to get you freed, and we can do it. But not without you.

Look at yourself: you're still alive! Isn't that amazing? Do you know how many people who are accused of blasphemy are stoned on the spot without any form of trial? You have had two trials, and we are doing everything we can to get you tried in front of the Supreme Court. You have to take this chance, Asia. Hang in there because, whether you want me to or not, I am going to keep going.

Sending you loving hugs,

Anne-Isabelle

I was touched and encouraged by her kindness, but the support and interest of the international community had not yielded any results. The High Court of Lahore showed no hesitation in wanting to kill me. I no longer hoped for anything.

Immediately following the trial, my prison conditions got tougher. I wasn't allowed family visits anymore, nor was I permitted the comforting presence of my guard, Mamita. For a few weeks, I remained in solitary confinement, where I had nothing to do but think about my looming death. Ashiq explained to me much later the reason for the changes: a Taliban commando tried to kill me inside the prison itself. Despite the barriers, they managed to get inside but were captured by the guards. The authorities found detonators, grenades, and explosive belts among their belongings. Also inside the terrorists' bags were highly detailed plans of the prison, on which my cell was marked with a red circle. They were on a mission to kill me. Even today, I cannot comprehend their relentlessness.

In solitary confinement, which is a waiting room for death, I sometimes prayed. *I experience no hatred against anyone. I do not hate those who made me suffer all these years. I forgive everyone and pray for those who hurt me.*

Seven weeks after my second death sentence came Christmas, which was difficult for us all. The warden reluctantly agreed to allow me to spend a bit of time with my family, and my daughters came with Ashiq and Joseph. But this time, our hearts were so very heavy. We were only allowed thirty minutes in the presence of two guards, who recorded everything we said to one another. Joseph read aloud a passage from the Bible, and then we cut up the cake, but our hearts were not in it. Before having to part again, I hugged my daughters tightly and told them that the best day of my life would be the day when I would be able to dry their tears.

"Don't abandon us, Mom," my little Eisha pleaded.

I feared dying, but I could no longer go on living this kind of existence. I could hold on for my children, but for how much longer? And where would I draw the strength and courage to fight and keep going? I felt battered by fate, and despite that, I still hoped for a happy ending. I prayed night and day, and God heard me. After a few weeks in isolation without any form of contact with anyone whatsoever, I returned to my cell, hoping Mamita was still my assigned guard. She was so joyful, generous, and above all, bigger and tougher than me. She had enough strength for the both of us.

At first, while we were getting to know each other, she explained to me that one of her nieces, Nour, had been thrown in jail because she didn't want to marry a Muslim man after he raped her. Nour, who was barely twenty years old, found herself in a cell with women who did not want to share space with a Christian woman. When Nour prayed to Jesus, her fellow inmates hit her, so she prayed at night, while the other women slept. The Lord must have helped her cellmates fall asleep quickly so that his child could adore him. She had a brief respite until she became subject to the brutal torture of the guardswoman, who relentlessly harassed her to convert to Islam. Nour never caved, but her heart did. It was one strike too many. After her niece died, Mamita decided to become a prison guard so that she could be a bit of comfort to prisoners, be they Muslims or Christians. For all my misery, Mamita and Nour helped me understand how fortunate I was to have a cell to myself.

When I saw Mamita walk through the door, I was so relieved that I celebrated aloud: "Thank you, God, for hearing my prayers."

Mamita responded with a wide grin. For a moment, she helped me forget where I was and why I was there. "I brought you a clean blanket, and in this bag, you'll find a little something for your Christmas. It is never too late to celebrate Jesus' birth."

Looking at the bag, I felt what my little Eisham must have experienced when she was given her first rag doll.

"Don't be shy, Asia, open it."

I plunged my hand into the bag and found a beautiful pair of socks, which I rushed to put on.

"Besides Ashiq, you are the first person to give me a present," I said. "Mamita, I prayed the Lord to give me a bit of hope back, but I wasn't expecting so much. Your gesture and your big heart overwhelm me. Thank you."

"Mind you, Asia, you must be very careful and hide your socks when the other guards come. I wouldn't want them to land you in more trouble. I have to leave you now. I have already spent too much time in your company."

Throughout the frozen January winter, Mamita's socks warmed both my feet and my heart. Thanks to her kindness, a bit of energy returned to me. Then, when my generous guard told me a week later that the Supreme Court had accepted my appeal, I was no longer defeated and sad but strong and combative.

Chapter 10

OUTSIDE MY PRISON

Democracy needs support,
and the best support for a democracy
comes from other democracies.
BENAZIR BHUTTO, SPEECH, 1989

With a new trial on the horizon that might overturn the previous verdicts, my execution was delayed again. From suspended sentence to suspended sentence, my life went on. When Ashiq and Joseph paid me a visit, I knew that they came bearing good news, and I was happy for them to see me in better shape both morally and physically. In the visiting room, I thought they looked tired, but they had big smiles on their faces.

"You see, Asia, all is not lost. On the contrary, the Supreme Court has agreed to review your entire judgment!" Ashiq announced, holding his chin high and proud.

"Yes, I heard from Mamita. She is optimistic, too, but I would rather remain prudent."

"You're right, Asia," Joseph burst out, "but bear in mind that if the Supreme Court is starting over from scratch, then they must think it's possible that the other judges made a mistake. It is a very good sign, you know."

"Yes, we'll see. I have been so disappointed in the past that I am now wary. And you, how are you? And the girls?"

Ashiq and Joseph avoided my gaze, and I suddenly felt very anxious. Ashiq clearly didn't want to answer me, so Joseph cleared his throat before recounting their harrowing story:

> The moon was shining over our Christian neighborhood, and Ashiq and I were calmly drinking our chai before bed. All of a sudden, a group of men started anxiously knocking on our metal door, shouting, "Open up!" We were gripped with fear and could sense that their intentions were not peaceful. All the children were sleeping upstairs with my wife, Amina. We climbed the steps as quickly as we could. The knocking had torn them from their sleep, and they all sat upright in bed. We could hear the men outside uttering terrifying insults: "You family of dogs! We're going to finish you off!"
>
> "Get dressed," I ordered, "we have to leave immediately!" Out on the street, the men hammered on, yelling even more: "He's a blasphemer! Death to him and his family! Don't let them get away!"

They managed to force the door open and found an empty house. We fled through the rooftops. Ever since your sentencing, Asia, I have not been at ease, so I always leave a ladder upstairs, just in case.

I was devastated. "And where are you living now?" I asked.

"My brother housed us for a bit," Joseph shared, "and then he helped us find a place. The next day, he was brave enough to go to our house and gather all our things."

"Ashiq, how did the girls get through all of this?"

"They were very scared that night, but now they are alright. They've even made some friends in our new neighborhood."

"Tell me, Joseph, who were those men and why were they specifically lashing out at you?"

"We are on Tehreek-e-Labbaik's radar, which is one of the most fanatical religious parties in the country. For one thing, they are proponents of the death penalty for blasphemy crimes, but they strongly support assassinating people who oppose the law. Since they failed to kill you in prison by combining forces with the Taliban, they are trying to hurt you by hurting us instead."

I was terrified for my family's safety, but I was also powerless. Before leaving them, I asked Joseph to write to Anne-Isabelle:

My friend,

Each of our lives contains a little poem that we don't always know how to express. But why does

God—he who knows all and sees all—leave me in this miserable cell? What is he waiting for to let me leave it? Thank you for not abandoning me and for continuing to take care of my family. I am going to fight too.

—Asia

When we met in Canada, Anne-Isabelle explained the challenges and doubts she experienced throughout my years of captivity. According to her, my case was a political bombshell in Pakistan. On the one hand, it seemed impossible that the political authorities would execute me given the international press, but on the other hand, she worried that all the media attention could also negatively affect my release by provoking the Islamists, who would intensely pressure the court to hang me. She explained that was probably why my trials were continually delayed. The international mobilization she roused could have also been counterproductive because it reinforced the prejudices of the Islamists that Christians are agents of the West who are waging a war on Islam, which is obviously not true. She also feared they would let me die slowly if too much time passed, so she made sure the newspapers talked about me regularly.

I had the hardest time understanding how anyone could think I was against Islam. I love my country and the Muslims who inhabit it! Thanks to Anne-Isabelle's explanations, it became easier for me to understand why people around the world would talk about me quite a bit and then sometimes not mention me at all. When the Supreme Court accepted to review my sentence, Anne-Isabelle made a lot of noise about it, and ultimately, I realize she used the same means as the Islamists to exert pressure on the judges but without violence.

I later found out that Anne-Isabelle started an organization bearing my name to collect money to help support my family and to pay for my defense. Then she wrote a second book about me titled *Death Is Not a Solution*.[13] I didn't know the contents of the book, but I certainly agreed with the title. With the help of several European congresspeople, she asked her country's parliament to impose financial sanctions on Pakistan if I was not freed. She also gave a second speech to the United Nations before launching an international online campaign called "A Glass of Water for Asia Bibi." The idea was simple: everyone who supported me took pictures of themselves drinking a glass of water in solidarity.

I told Anne-Isabelle that of all the pictures I had seen of her online, the one with the glass of water was by far my favorite. My family and daughters also played along. Ashiq and Joseph reported back that they had fun taking pictures of each other one afternoon, and they were touched when they saw on the computer that people from around the world were drinking large glasses of water to show their support. I didn't expect so many

---

13   La Mort n'est pas une solution, March 2015, Éditions du Rocher.

people to rally around my story, and it felt good to know that my cause did not leave the international community indifferent.

Mamita was never afraid to tell me the truth about what was going on. She knew my family didn't tell me everything in order to protect me, but she felt that I could handle it since she was supporting me on a daily basis. She explained that although a lot of people were talking about me in foreign newspapers, our country was much more interested in the fate of Mumtaz Qadri, the man who had assassinated Governor Taseer and was sentenced to death for his crime. Mamita also briefly described to me what was happening in the streets.

It was not until I left prison that my lawyer, Saif ul-Malook, who served as the prosecutor in Qadri's case, explained everything to me in detail: "A month after he assassinated Governor Taseer, Mumtaz Qadri answered to two counts of indictment before the courts: one for terrorism and one for murder. At the end of the closed hearing, I asked for capital punishment, and the judges followed my recommendation by sentencing him to death by hanging, the same sentence they gave you. The investigation revealed that the bodyguard decided to follow through with the murder four days after listening to an *imam*'s sermon that called for the deaths of blasphemers. In condemning Qadri like this, the Pakistani courts sent a strong signal to other clergymen calling for the murders of people accused of blasphemy. Though to be fair, the judges fled our country after announcing that verdict, fearing reprisals from Qadri's supporters. After the sentencing, which also fined Qadri two hundred thousand rupees, the murderer's lawyer immediately appealed the court's decision."

I hadn't killed anyone! Not only had I received the same death sentence, but my fine was also three times greater than the murderer's—three hundred thousand rupees!

"And would you believe it, Asia," Saif continued, "the criminal continued to spill blood from within his prison. Qadri radicalized one of his guards. In September 2013, a guard at Adiyala prison in the suburbs of Islamabad opened fire on Mohammad Asghar, who was seventy years old and suffered from schizophrenia. He had been sentenced to death for having written letters in which he claimed to be a prophet. The guard who tried to kill him confessed that he had been receiving religious lessons from Qadri. Later, an internal report from the prison concluded that he tried to radicalize other guards in order to persuade them to shoot inmates accused or convicted of blasphemy. What is even more unfair, Asia, is that unlike you, Qadri enjoyed favorable treatment in prison. The staff never raised their voices at him. They spoke to him with respect and spared him the daily chores.

"With his appeal, his death sentencing was suspended in March 2015 before it was confirmed by the Supreme Court a few months later. Qadri hanged on the morning of Monday, February 29, but you know our country. Religious leaders called their supporters to express their anger in the wake of the execution. And if you remember, that was when you were put into solitary confinement again. I requested that you be placed there for your safety. The *mullahs* were drawing the link between you and Qadri, since he had been hanged for killing the governor who defended you. I knew isolation was hard for you, but I don't regret my decision.

"Immediately after the hanging, the country went into a state of alert, and I feared something might happen to you from within the prison. That same day, several huge gatherings simultaneously took place in the major cities, both to protest the execution of Qadri and to demand you be hanged. For two days, entire neighborhoods were closed off, and the highway between the capital and the airport was shut down. Lawyers went on strike, and schools closed their doors. You have to realize, even if it is a bit complicated, that while Islamists saw Qadri as a hero, hundreds of progressive Pakistanis on Twitter celebrated the historic day when the justice system did its job without succumbing to religious pressure.

"Mumtaz Qadri was buried in a mausoleum in Bara Haku, a neighborhood on the outskirts of the capital, but since then, his tomb has become a site of pilgrimage. His remains lay in a white marble tomb with four slender minarets and a green-tiled dome above it. Every year since his hanging, an *urs*—a Muslim ceremony like the kind that takes place to honor the holy *Sufis* in Pakistan—gathers hundreds of thousands of people, the very same people who wish to see you hanged. While the government showed unexpected resolve in applying the ultimate sentence, it did nothing to prevent the construction of the sanctuary that glorifies Governor Taseer's murderer. In my mind, the fact that the sanctuary exists is a comfort to those who support the blasphemy law. It is practically a call to murder!"

Everything Saif was saying baffled me. "But with this sanctuary, isn't it like he is beatified?" I asked.

"It is exactly like that, Asia," he answered, "and I was shocked that the government did not so much as raise an eyebrow when the governor's murderer received such an honor, as if he were a national hero. That is why I agreed to defend you. I did so both in memory of the governor and to fight against all forms of Islamist extremism—through you."

"I hope the Vatican will do something for the Federal Minister for Minorities Affairs, Shahbaz Bhatti, who killed no one but gave his life in the name of justice," I said.

"I am sure the Christians will be able to distinguish between good and evil because, honestly, our society couldn't sink to a lower level of morality. To pay homage to a bodyguard who killed the man he was charged to protect and who was deemed a terrorist by the highest court in Pakistan..."

Saif's face flushed redder and redder with anger, and then he lowered his voice, adding, "But you see, Asia, I defended you, and we won."

Saif also helped me win the battle to have a Bible while in prison. He and the warden exchanged numerous letters on the subject, and the warden eventually caved. I was allowed to use the tiny Bible that Ashiq brought back from Rome for me, provided I was discreet. Mamita was kind enough to help me read it, or rather read it to me. That Bible was our little treasure; it was engraved inside us. To prepare to face another year in solitude, I also recited the prayer that Pope Francis gave me: "Christ forgave us," I repeated to myself, "and I, too, must pardon those who hurt me. Father, forgive them, for they know not what they do."

I was always happy to see Mamita. I could be myself with her without having to worry about being misinterpreted or misunderstood in a way that would lead to beatings or yet another conviction. Unlike other guards, she would unlock and close the door to my cell gently. She also brought me the raw ingredients for my meals. Since Kadeeja's firing, I was responsible for my own cooking and washing, and I prepared them in my one and only dish in my cell. My family, Saif, and Anne-Isabelle insisted on it, fearing I might be poisoned. I was grateful for these tasks that kept me fairly busy during the day. Mamita would find a way to stay longer than she was supposed to, but we had to be careful. She provided me with great moral support between these walls, and after what happened to Bouguina, I couldn't stand the thought of losing my one and only ally in this prison.

When Easter was approaching, Mamita helped me as I tried to obtain permission for a bishop to come to my cell and give me Holy Communion. The bishop agreed, but the warden did not authorize it. I was disappointed, but I was still more lively than usual on Easter morning, even though Ashiq would not be visiting me. Easter is such a joyful celebration, and it brought a bit of hope to my life in my subterranean cell. It was early in the day, and I knew Mamita would soon bring me a jar of water because she always came after the second morning prayer. I hoped she would have tea with me on this special day for us.

I had my loveliest smile ready for Mamita, but I swallowed it as soon as I saw her face. She wore a dull expression that seemed to contain all the sadness in the world. It was a look I'd never seen on her before. I concluded that something horrendous must have happened, and my heart did not feel strong enough to bear more bad news. Mamita said nothing as she set the jar of water next to me.

"What's wrong, Mamita?"

She seemed deeply afflicted. After hesitating for a moment, she answered me in a weak, barely audible voice: "Something terrible happened last night in Lahore. An attack aimed at our Christian brothers and sisters killed more than seventy-two people, including twenty-nine children and six women."

My heart felt as if it were in the clutches of a crushing hand. "But I don't understand," I said, confused. "Where and when did this happen?"

"The attack happened in Gulshan-e-Iqbal park in Lahore at around six-thirty p.m. A suicide bomber packed to the brim with explosives blew himself up by a children's merry-go-round near the park's entrance."

Horror gripped my throat, making it difficult to speak. "I

know the place very well. Ashiq and I took the children there several times and picnicked to celebrate Easter."

"It is all they are talking about on TV. The images show women and children in pools of blood, screaming and crying. Witnesses said that when the explosion happened, bodies flew through the air, and the flames rose so high they were taller than the trees."

"Mamita, you have always told me the truth," I could barely whisper, "was it because of me?"

She winced and swallowed hard. "They were able to identify the man behind the attack because they found his head. He was twenty-eight years old. A few hours after the massacre, the Taliban claimed it and said they were targeting Christians."

"Oh my God," I said, horrified. "But you haven't answered my question, Mamita. Was it because of my story?"

"It's difficult to say. Ever since Qadri was hanged, the Christian community has been expecting backlash. At Mass this morning, my parish's priest said in his sermon that the attack was not a surprise and that security measures were clearly insufficient around churches and places where Christians congregate. We feared something like this might happen, especially since the Islamists scheduled commemorative prayers for Qadri today—on Easter. So it wasn't directly linked to your story, at least not completely. However, the attack took place while thousands of Qadri supporters clashed with police, demanding your execution."

I collapsed onto my bed and gasped for air. The walls of the prison felt like they were cracking and collapsing on top of me.

"You are not responsible for the madness of men, Asia!" Mamita insisted. "Your case is going to create a precedent here because the entire world knows you and is watching Pakistan closely. I very much believe in you, and your story is going to help our country move toward the light."

She took my shoulders in her strong, gentle hands. "Come on, catch your breath," she said softly. "You are not allowed to give up. Let us pray for all those unhappy people. Many Muslims were among the victims. Let us pray that God welcomes them into heaven. Let us cry for our victims, console ourselves, and learn to love one another again so that Pakistan and every other nation can restore hope. To get through this tragedy, let us entrust the lost souls to the Lord, who comforts those who grieve." She bowed her head. "Jesus, Lord, grant them rest. Grant them eternal rest."

Then Mamita pulled out a white cloth that was wrapped around a piece of a consecrated wafer, which she kept and hid after receiving Communion earlier that morning. My eyes misted with emotion.

"Oh! Thank you! Thank you, Mamita, for this offering. What you did for me is so beautiful."

"Quieter, Asia," Mamita whispered as she leaned in toward me. "The guards have sensitive ears."

I kept the wafer in my mouth for as long as I could, and

once I swallowed it, the Body of Christ brought a warmth that spread throughout my body.

Other key events happened as more months went by, and I learned how to process the good news with the bad news and handle challenges as they came. One morning, Ashiq proudly announced that a poster with my portrait was on display, front and center, at the Hôtel de Ville, the Paris City Hall. It was hard to believe that the French capital took such an interest in my fate; I who was so far away in the depths of Punjab! Ashiq and Joseph, all smiles, showed me a picture that Anne-Isabelle had taken of the poster in front of the historic building. It was astounding to think of all the people I didn't know who would see the poster, which bore the words "Freedom for Asia Bibi" in French.

"Tell me, Ashiq, why is it that people always show that particular photograph of me? I was only twenty-five at the time, and now I am over fifty."

"Do you remember when Anne-Isabelle was still living in Pakistan, and she came over to our house when your sister still lived there, and Anne-Isabelle asked if she could take that photo? She put it on the cover of your first book, and the media has been using it ever since."

"If I get out of here one day, nobody will recognize me," I said. "Or everyone will find me ugly and damaged."

"No, Asia," Joseph assured me. "People need easy reference points, and that photograph makes you instantly recognizable. It's very good."

"Plus, it's your soul they love, not your age," Ashiq added confidently.

Other cities in France,[14] as well as cities in Spain and Italy, displayed the same picture. I told Ashiq it would be good for him to write a letter to the mayor of Paris to thank her for having been the first to do so. Ashiq and Joseph agreed.

November 18, 2014

Mrs. Mayor,

I have just returned from Multan prison, where my wife, Asia Bibi, was transferred several months ago. Ever since she was sentenced to death in 2010 for drinking water in the well of our village, we have lived in fear. Our family is under constant threat. The children and I live in hiding as close to her as we can because she needs us to give her a reason to keep living and fighting.

After four long years of waiting and living under very difficult conditions, we hoped that the High Court of Lahore would free her. She did not commit blasphemy, and she never said anything blasphemous. Ever since the High Court confirmed my wife's death sentence, we have not been able to understand why the Pakistan we love is lashing out against us. Our family has always been happy here, and we never had problems with anybody. We are Christian, and

14 Bordeaux, Le Mans, La Flèche, La Brède.

we respect Islam. Our neighbors are Muslim, and we lived among them in our little village. But in the past few years, the situation has changed, and we are afraid. Many of our Muslim friends are also unable to understand why the Pakistani justice system imposes such suffering on our family. We are currently rallying to win our final appeal, which was submitted to the Supreme Court, but we are also aware that the best way out of this would be to obtain a presidential pardon. We wholeheartedly believe that she will not be hanged if the venerable President of Pakistan, Mamnoon Hussain, grants her forgiveness.

No one should die over a glass of water. Thanks to a handful of local friends who risk their lives to protect us, our children and I are able to survive by being very cautious. And thanks to Anne-Isabelle Tollet, who became our sister four years ago and with whom we speak very often, we receive news of all of the people who have rallied for us around the world. It means so much to us. It helps us hold on to hope. Every time I visit Asia, I tell her about it. Sometimes, it helps make her brave again.

A few days ago, I found out that you have offered to welcome us if my wife is able to get out of prison. What an honor! I would like to thank you, Mrs. Mayor, and tell you how much respect and gratitude we have for you. I hope we will be able to make it to you alive.

Yesterday, when I went to see Asia, she asked me to pass on this message to you: "In my small, windowless cell, days and nights resemble one another, but if I am still standing, it is thanks to you all. My heart is warmed every time Ashiq shows me pictures of people drinking glasses of water and thinking of me. I have heard that the city of Paris welcomes us. I want to thank everyone in Paris and the mayor. You are my only chance of escaping the depths of this prison. Please don't let me down. I did not commit blasphemy."

—Ashiq Masih

Anne-Isabelle made sure the world read my letter. It felt like I was sending a message in a bottle out to sea, but it seemed to initiate a landslide around the world. All of the major newspapers in every continent agreed to publish the letter, and my name became more and more well known. Mamita reported that millions of people signed petitions to help finally set me free!

Chapter 11

ACQUITTED...REALLY?

Justice is the penalty for established injustices.
Anatole France, *L'Affaire Crainquebille*

I left my cell one day to answer a phone call. Like every other time such an event occurred, so unexpected and sudden, I felt torn between the mad hope of a positive outcome and the terror of having to face more bad news. Trembling, I took hold of the receiver that a guard held out to me.

"Hello, Asia?"

"Yes..."

"It's Saif ul-Malook, your lawyer. Can you hear me?"

I held my breath and said nothing.

"I am honored to tell you that you have just been acquitted by the Supreme Court."

"What?"

"You are now a free human being."

"Excuse me?"

"You can take off and go wherever you please."

"But...did that really happen? Are you sure this isn't a mistake?"

"No, I assure you. The judges have just acquitted you this very moment."

I would not allow myself to believe it. "What did you say for them to finally recognize my innocence?"

"I am still in court. I must leave you to sign some papers."

"Wait! Please. Don't give me false hope."

"I repeat, you are innocent in the eyes of Pakistani justice."

"I'm...free? Really?"

"I have to hang up now, but I will tell you all the details later."

"Wait, don't hang up. When are you going to pick me up? Hello? Hello, are you there?" I couldn't hear anyone on the other end. I said thank you, but he had already hung up.

I was completely floored and dumbfounded by this revelation. I couldn't believe it, or rather, I would not allow myself to hope that it was true. I couldn't picture leaving this place or imagine that it was possible to leave it. When I was taken back to my cell, I lay down like a robot on my bed as if the call hadn't happened. Was this a new trap being laid out for me? Alone in my own little world, confusion began to settle in my mind. The lawyer had spoken so fast, and I hadn't been able to hear him well. Was this a miracle, *my* miracle? *Lord, speak to me,* I prayed.

Hours went by, and I knew I would not be able to calm down until I was truly out of there. A lot of people wanted me dead, including many inside that very prison. The pressure of the past ten years fell slowly, little by little. Overcome with exhaustion, I fell asleep.

"Asia. Asia, wake up."

Mamita gently shook me until I opened my eyes. I felt dazed and depressed, as if I had slept forever, but my mind lit up again when I realized Mamita was standing over me. I read the worry in her eyes.

"You have been sleeping nonstop for three days," she said. "I was starting to worry about you. Do you feel alright?"

"Yes," I whispered, struggling to sit up in my *charpai.*

"Here, take this cup of tea. I put a lot of sugar in it. You need it."

With every sip, I felt myself coming around. Then, I was suddenly overwhelmed with anxiety.

"Mamita, was I declared not guilty, or did I dream it?"

Helping herself to a cup of hot tea, Mamita smiled. "You were acquitted, Asia. Now you are free."

"But if I am free to go and breathe the air from somewhere other than here, then why am I still in this cell?"

She frowned. "Ever since you were acquitted by the judges, let's just say that...well, it's hardly news to you that your case is a bit of a special one. While you were asleep, some things happened in our country that relate to you, and it is all they are talking about on TV."

Mamita told me that as soon as my acquittal was announced,

Tehreek-e-Labbaik Pakistan (TLP), an Islamist group known for its particularly hard line when it came to blasphemy, organized huge demonstrations in protest.

"They demand that you be hanged along with the judges who acquitted you, who they're also calling blasphemers," Mamita explained. "While you have been asleep over these past three days, the country has become totally paralyzed. All of the major roads in the country have been closed to traffic, including the highway that leads to the airport. People have remained in their homes, fearing the rage of the Islamists. Many businesses and schools are closed, and the phone network remains cut off for a good part of the day in the major cities. The clerics said before the crowd: 'Freeing Asia is the first step toward repealing the blasphemy law. The West has always tried to change it, but we will resist.'"

Frightened by what I was hearing, I stared at Mamita.

"You're pale, Asia. Do you want me to stop?"

"No, no, keep going. I need to know, even if it is unpleasant. I am worried about my family. I hope they are all in a safe place."

"They have always managed very well. It's sad to say, but they are used to having to hide. It will be alright. Don't worry."

"You are probably right, Mamita. Tell me more about what is happening."

Mamita then told me that another demonstration leader was calling for the army to mutiny. But on TV that same evening, the spokesperson for the army said that this was a judicial matter that had nothing to do with the army. He hammered at the point, saying, "Don't drag us into this sort of business."

Faced with these threats, Pakistani Prime Minister Imran Khan called for the people to respect the Supreme Court's decision. In a solemn TV appearance, the head of state asked his compatriots to ignore those who called for a rejection of the verdict. He said they were doing so in their own political interest and not doing Islam any favors. He said their language was that of the enemies of Pakistan. "Don't force us to act," he added, addressing those who encouraged violence in the country.

"Many Pakistanis, and I am the first among them," Mamita went on, "welcomed his firm tone, even if we also worried about the chaos that would set in. We could tell the authorities were overwhelmed and hesitant to intervene because the government feared a violent reaction."

With a lump in her throat, Mamita told me that I might be tried once more. The news tore my heart to pieces, and despite my best efforts, I was unable to hide my despair.

"But how is that possible? My lawyer told me he wasn't messing with me! Oh, it was too good to be true!"

Mamita tried to calm me down by telling me that Prime Minister Imran Khan negotiated with the Islamists to reestablish order. She also reminded me that I mustn't forget that the prime minister was ultimately on my side and knew what he was doing when he signed the agreement, which involved accepting a "review application" for my trial.

"What does that mean, Mamita? Am I going to be tried again? Does the Supreme Court's verdict no longer count?"

"It means that in order to to get the Islamists to calm down, the Supreme Court is going to make sure they didn't make any mistakes and that they are certain of their decision."

"So they could change their minds?"

"Or not! They can also say: 'We did indeed check, and we are sure of Asia Bibi's innocence, so there is no point in having a new trial.' Have faith, Asia, it is almost over."

The *imam* from my village submitted the review application. He was clearly unwilling to give up despite the fact that he wasn't even present during the fight with the women in the harvest field.

After Mamita left, I knelt down in my cell and prayed to God:

My God, help me find the right words. I am broken, crushed, completely exhausted. My heart roars. Lord, all of my desire is laid out before you, and none of my complaints escape you. I haven't the heart, my strength is failing me, and even the light in my eyes is fading. Those who want my death hound me. Those people who want me to suffer are speaking evil words. I am keeping my mouth shut, and Lord, I know that you will respond. My enemies are strong and vigorous, and a lot of them have it out for me. When I look for goodness, they accuse me. My God,

*never abandon me. Do not stray far from me. Come
quickly to my aid.*

Saif visited me the following day, and he immediately
brought up the review application, assuring me it didn't hold up:
"It is a trick from the government to get the Islamists to calm
down because foreigners continue to extend discreet invitations
for you to come to their countries. But as long as the application
hasn't been examined, you can't leave Pakistan."

"Will all of this never end? That could take years again!"

"The world is watching us. It will happen fast."

I was slightly reassured by Saif, who seemed confident.
I told myself that he had managed the impossible, and I was
curious to know what he said to the judges for them to finally
acknowledge my innocence.

As he had promised on the phone, he took his time explaining everything to me: "My strategy was to show that you had
been the victim of a conspiracy, and the judges heard me. The
decision, which was signed by Saqib Nisar, the first president of
the Supreme Court, was fifty-six pages long and explained the
motivations behind your acquittal. I'll tell you the key points.

"The alleged blasphemy incident took place on June 14,
2009. However, the first complaint was submitted on June 19,
2009, that is, five days later. That delay, according to legal precedent, was indicative of a conspiracy. The two women who were
eyewitnesses, Mafia and her sister, fought with you and said you
had made blasphemous statements about Muhammad in front

of at least twenty-five to thirty women, but no other women appeared before the court to support the claim. Another woman declared in her deposition that the dispute was not related to a source of drinking water even though she had said that it was in other statements. So there was a real contradiction.

"The eyewitnesses stated that one thousand people from the village had been present at the assembly to incriminate you before the local *imams*, while other people mentioned only one hundred people and referred to another location. There are contradictory versions of the story, including details about the duration of the assembly. The Court, having noted numerous inconsistencies, decided that it was not possible to confirm beyond any reasonable doubt that Asia Bibi was guilty. You were, therefore, acquitted of all charges made against you."

Joy surged through me at hearing the truth finally come out, but I still didn't understand the trial review. "Can you explain to me how it is possible that I would be tried again after all of that?"

Saif's cellphone began to ring in his pocket, and he apologized for having to answer the call. "Yes, understood," he said into the phone. "I will do what is needed." He put his phone away and gave me a big smile. "You are going to be leaving your prison, Asia. Tomorrow at the latest. It has all been arranged."

"I am really going to leave? I am going to reunite with my family?"

"No, not exactly," he started. "First, you will meet your husband in Islamabad, but your children will stay in Lahore with

Joseph. As long as the court has not reviewed your trial, you will remain in a safe place so that you aren't killed. And if the judges ever decide to try you again, which seems quite unlikely to me, then you will return to prison."

"Why, that's horrible! How can they do that to me? I have to go on living with the anxiety of being hanged. Because if they decide to try me again, it would only be to hang me. Otherwise there would be no point."

"Everything in its own time, Asia. Focus on the good news: you are getting out of prison, and for the time being, you are no longer guilty of anything. I am going to fly to Europe because, since your acquittal, the Isalmists have been looking for me, and it is too dangerous for me to live here now. I would like to stay, but they are forcing me to leave."

Panic rose in my chest. "But if you aren't here, they are going to convict me all over again!"

"I won't be leaving you. I will monitor your situation from Europe, and I am telling you again, Asia, I am very confident. Now, I have to set up your release before leaving myself. I'll say goodbye to you for now, and I ask to you to continue to believe. You know the hardest part is behind you."

Heading back to my cell, I found the place less dark and less bleak than usual. I told myself that if I wasn't totally innocent, they wouldn't allow me to leave the prison, and that knowledge calmed me down. Lying on my *charpai*, I thought back to my first night in prison and to the nine years that followed, with their moments of hope and despair. To my cruel guards, like Khalil and Kadeeja, and to those who had been kind and gentle, like Bouguina and Mamita. With a heavy heart, I would say goodbye to Mamita the following morning.

When night fell, I heard an unusual commotion. Men were running, calling out to each other, and yelling. Gates opened and closed, and footsteps hurried down the hallway. Fear gripped me when I recognized the sound of the bootsteps stomping toward my cell. Terrified, I cried out "Mamita!"

My door slammed open to reveal Khalil, the guardian from my first prison. He stared at me with bloodshot eyes: "As soon as I heard the news, I found a way to get here. Did you really think you were going to get out of it that easy?"

I completely froze and then cried out, "But you've made a mistake! You must know the judges said I wasn't guilty."

"Sure, you were acquitted, but we decided otherwise. Your lawyer, the judges, and even the prime minister aren't the ones making the rules now! They're corrupted by the West and betraying Islam. I am here to put things back in order, and I guarantee you will never leave this prison."

His boots rushed forward and then, overtaken with rage, he grabbed me by the hair and yanked my head back. My headscarf slid onto the ground, and as he stomped, he spat, "You aren't even presentable. You will remain unworthy until the end, when you go to hell."

As I begged him to spare me, he bound my hands with a piece of rope that cut into my flesh.

"You're coming with me, you filthy vermin!"

"I beg you, please!"

He grabbed the rope to drag me out of bed, slammed the door behind us, and covered my mouth with his hand. With beastly strength, he dragged me down the hallway. My blood ran cold, and I couldn't see anything—neither the ground nor the walls. Nothing except the small door under the stairway that led to the exercise area. The door opened onto a spiral staircase that led to the basement. I tried to resist by braking with my feet, but he pulled on the rope that held my hands together with all his might. We started down the stairs, and I tripped over a rusty step. I fell down and barely caught myself. Khalil wasn't slowing down. I knew this descent was leading me to the end.

I cried and shouted, "Help me!"

Khalil turned around and kicked me in the thigh with his boot before dragging me into a vaulted room. The humidity of the basement was suffocating, and an intolerable smell of spoilt meat made me gag.

"You can feel death, can't you," the guard mocked sadistically.

I scanned the dark room, lit only by two torches. On the ceiling, a bat hung upside down above a worn noose. I realized I, too, would hang soon. On the ground rested an empty apple crate.

I screamed, "Don't do this!"

Khalil responded by kicking my lower back. The smell of death made me want to throw up.

"You're scared, aren't you? Well, you should be because your time has come!"

"Wait, ask the warden! You can't do this!"

I knew I was going to be killed, but I didn't want to die with Khalil. A burning thirst dried out my chest. As he pulled me up to stand on the crate, I said my prayers to the Lord and prayed for my children. While Khalil adjusted the length of the noose, I asked the Lord why he had inflicted so much suffering on me, why he had let barbarians win. I would have rather been killed ten years ago to have prevented the deaths of the governor and the minister and to spare my family of all the grief. I thought about the people around the world who supported me. All of their time and effort just to wind up hanging from this noose in the basement of a prison, and by Khalil's hand!

"I beg you! I'm innocent!"

Putting the noose around my neck, Khalil responded to my plea with a cackle, but I couldn't hear him any more than I could my heart, which spoke to me. I stopped struggling. I stopped thinking about anything. My mind was blank. Khalil grumbled, unable to size the noose correctly to fit my neck.

"And to think that I have to do the work myself," he complained while fussing with the rope. My fear drowned out most of his words. "I'm a guard, not an executioner. Your family and the judges...Bye-bye, parasites...*Allah Akbar*!"

He tested the strength of the worn rope. With each passing second, I felt life slowly leaving my body and the beginning of death. I was dying while still alive. And then I felt the discomfort of the rope. Khalil pushed me off the crate and into the void. A dry snap sounded as the rope became taut, and I kicked the air like a puppet. My body spasmed as my legs desperately searched for a foothold. Then, little by little, my muscles relaxed, and I felt my bladder empty. Khalil watched me with a huge grin on his face, and I smiled back at him before dying.

Sunlight poured through the window and illuminated the room to produce a setting similar to how I imagined heaven to look. I heard whispers and the sounds of washing dishes. My body was crippled with pain and tremendous fatigue. The smell of toast wafted toward my nostrils. When I heard Ashiq's soft voice, I thought I was dreaming.

"Asia! Asia, calm down!"

My body was curled into a ball, and a hand caressed my hair. I clutched onto it tightly with both of mine.

"Are you awake?"

I dripped with sweat, and my head hurt. "Wait, what are you doing here? Where are we?" I asked.

"You were freed from prison last night. You had a restless night of sleep. You must have had a nightmare."

I sat up in the unfamiliar bed and felt something cold and wet between my legs.

"Everything is going to be fine now."

"I was hanged last night. It was Khalil. It seemed so real."

"It was only a nightmare," Ashiq assured me, taking my hand, which trembled like a leaf. "Don't you remember last night? We came to get you in your cell, and we took a small plane to get here."

I looked up at the ceiling, which was painted salmon pink.

"You have everything you need here. You can shower and change, and we'll talk later."

"Yes, because my memory fails me. I remember my dream but not reality. What about our daughters? Where are they? Why aren't they here with us?"

"For security reasons, they are with Joseph, who is preparing all the papers. He has to leave as soon as possible. We are stuck here until your appeal is reexamined. The request of your accuser, Qari Muhammad Salam, will be examined by the Supreme Court on January 19. Three months from now."

"But that's ages away!"

"Yes, but you are no longer in prison, Asia. We are finally back together. That is a big step! Look how far we have come."

After taking a hot shower and gobbling down a few toasted *chapatis*, memories of the night before slowly came back to me. A flash of a small plane with a few foreigners and some Pakistani policemen on board. I thought of Mamita and felt immense grief at not having the chance to say goodbye to her. Given the circumstances, I knew she wouldn't be upset with me, and knowing her, she must have rejoiced that I finally made it out of my cell.

I remembered my ears hurting a lot on the plane. I had the distinct memory of a policeman holding out a helmet for me and explaining that is was to lessen the pressure and pain in my ears. And he was right. Wearing the helmet made the buzzing in my head stop and the journey less painful.

Ashiq explained to me that immediately following the Supreme Court's announcement of my acquittal, a Christian organization in London received him, Joseph, and the girls.

"It was a chance to tell the international community that we were in danger in Pakistan and couldn't live there without the risk of being killed," he said. "I recorded a message for Donald Trump, the president of the United States, asking them to grant us asylum. Eisham cried a lot and told journalists that she was very happy that the court finally recognized your innocence but that now she wanted to see you and give you a hug."

"Ashiq, I have thought nothing but that for thirty-five hundred days."

My husband tried to cheer me up by telling me that everyone abroad was pleased with the verdict. "Long live Pakistan," Salman Taseer's son, Shahbaz, tweeted. From the Vatican, Paul Bhatti, the brother of the murdered minister Shahbaz, said that my liberation "reflects the courage of the current courts and of the country, which is moving towards pacifist coexistence and respect for minorities." The international support gave us great hope even though we feared there might initially be repercussions against Christians.

There was a television in our small room, and I asked Ashiq if we could turn it on. I wanted to see what was being said on the news and find out if people were still talking about my case. On the Geo News channel, they happened to be broadcasting a press conference that Saif was holding in Europe:

> The verdict shows that poor people, minorities, and the more modest part of society are able to obtain justice in this country in spite of its flaws. I am happy that Asia Bibi was acquitted. This is the greatest and happiest day of my life. Prime Minister Imran Khan's government seems determined to ensure the safety of Asia, of her husband, Ashiq Masih, and of the couple's two daughters, until another country is willing to grant them asylum. Canada seems like their most likely destination...
>
> Asia is not a sophisticated person. She was born around fifty-four years ago to a poor family from a dusty village of farmers in the Punjab Province, and she never sat down in a classroom in her whole life, not even for one day. But she was sustained by her strong religious faith when she was faced with these blasphemy laws, which are often exploited by religious extremists and regular Pakistanis in order to

sort out personal disputes…Asia had never ventured far from her village before she found herself in prison, and so starting a new life in a new country might be a challenge for her. But she has demonstrated remarkable resilience throughout this whole ordeal, and I am sure that she will be up to the challenge.

"If you like," Ashiq said, "we can call Joseph and the girls. Do you feel ready?"

"Oh, yes!"

Ashiq called Joseph to let him know I was free and doing well. Joseph assured him that he and the girls were also safe although taking extra precautions because of the danger and the riots breaking out all over the country since my release. Joseph and Ashiq discussed the arrangements Anne-Isabelle had made for us all to take asylum in Canada. It was a place we could not even imagine, but we were joyful to receive the welcome of the president.

Finally, I could stand it no longer. "The girls!" I said, tugging on Ashiq's arm.

He laughed. "Yes, Joseph says they are jumping up and down to talk to you."

He handed me the phone.

"Hello, Mom?"

It was the sweetest sound I had ever heard.

Chapter 12

FREE AT LAST

*To deny any person their human rights
is to challenge their very humanity.*
NELSON MANDELA, ADDRESS TO U.S. CONGRESS, 1990

The months that followed are a period of my life that I don't care to remember much: morose, boring, useless time lived out under pressure and in a new sort of captivity. Ashiq and I were constantly swinging between emotions, either bursting with hope or beset with anguish, and it rhythmed our days. We both remained locked up in a room with a small kitchen and a bathroom, a sort of gilded prison whose doors only ever opened for us to receive food deliveries.

Seated in the hills outside Islamabad, the house we stayed in was under severe military protection. We were treated very well, but we circled around and around like fish trapped inside a bowl while we waited for the Supreme Court to decide whether or not to try me again. Under the guards' supervision, I was allowed to call my daughters once a day, no more. I felt terribly frustrated and afflicted that we were unable to celebrate Christmas 2018 together in Canada. It should have been the happiest Christmas of them all since I was recently freed and declared innocent. Instead, what a sad Christmas it was, with a judgment hanging over me with the possibility of being convicted yet again.

Ashiq, my daughters, and I held our breath for three long months before the Supreme Court delivered its conclusions. On Tuesday, January 29, the judges officially rejected the application for a trial review submitted by *Imam* Qari Salaam, who originally submitted the complaint. Saif announced the final verdict to me over the phone, but Ashiq and I did not let out true sighs of relief until we heard Judge Asif Saeed Khosa formally announce my acquittal to the world on live TV.

"Is this the face of Islam that we want to show the world?" the president of the Supreme Court intoned before a packed room. "Does Islam say that we should hang someone even if that person's guilt is not proven?"

Prior to the announcement of the courageous verdict and in order to avoid more riots throughout the country, Prime Minister Imran Khan made sure to put Khadim Hussain Rizvi, the leader of the Tehreek-e-Labbaik Pakistan (TLP) Islamist party, in jail along with three hundred of his followers on charges of rebellion and terrorism. They were responsible for setting up violent demonstrations and demanding my death in addition to the deaths of the judges when my acquittal was first announced. Now I could finally breathe. I was free, truly free, and in theory, nothing was keeping me in this country where Islamists threatened me with death.

I told my daughters over the phone, "It is only a matter of hours or a few days, sweeties. Get ready! Mommy and Daddy are hurrying to you!" At the end of the day, guards arrived to accompany us to the airport. I was so happy to finally unfurl my wings and fly to my children, although I felt terrible sadness that I would not have the opportunity to say goodbye to my dad.

Ashiq and I waited in an enclosed room in Benazir Bhutto International Airport under the protection of a guard who stood outside the door. Our only luggage was a plastic bag that held soap and a change of clothes. We were hopping up and down, impatient to board the plane of deliverance, when a military man wearing a black beret informed us it was time that we were off to Karachi.

"But—we are supposed to go to Canada to go find our children. This must be a mistake!"

"I can't tell you anything more. Those are the orders I received, and that is how it's going to be."

Ashiq and I looked at each other, completely bewildered. Tears welled up in my eyes when I asked the guard, "Why must I remain in Pakistan any longer? This is a nightmare! This can't be real!"

And yet it was real. After an hour-long flight, we found ourselves double-locked inside a squalid room on the second floor of a house guarded by the military in the port city of Karachi. In a stroke of luck, I was immediately granted permission to call Aman, my Pakistani friend, who worked for the European Union from Australia. He, too, was in shock and didn't understand why I wasn't permitted to leave the country when the Information Minister proclaimed everywhere that I was free to go wherever I pleased within Pakistan and abroad. What worried Aman was that the agreement that the government signed with the TLP, in addition to not opposing the review for application of the judgment, placed my name on a list that prevented me from leaving the country. This explained why I was still stuck in Pakistan.

Like wolves unwilling to release their prey, the Islamists persisted in attacking me. In turns, I felt weariness, anger, sadness, and anxiety. Ashiq was deeply distressed because he, too, was now imprisoned. I wished he could have gone to find our daughters instead. How time dragged on! Life moved as if it were in slow motion.

Thankfully, Aman helped me feel better each day over the phone. "You have to believe, Asia! You should know that a European Union congressman is currently in Islamabad and arranging your departure. His name is Jan Figel, and you can trust him."

"I don't believe anymore, Aman," I confessed. "I don't think I will ever see my daughters again. If I am assassinated or if something happens to me, please don't forget my children."

"I know it's hard, but you have to be patient a little while longer. I promise you will be reunited with your daughters."

How could I be patient after having lost almost ten years of my life over false accusations? And how was I supposed to accept that I still could not live freely when I had been definitively declared innocent? It made no sense. *Lord Jesus*, I prayed, *help me and stay with me. Now and forever.*

It is only in hindsight, and with Aman and Anne-Isabelle's help, that I understand why I remained stuck in Karachi for four months with Ashiq. According to Anne-Isabelle, the Islamists considered my departure a victory for the West, which was responsible for weakening blasphemy laws in Pakistan. Aman thought the Pakistani government was attempting to bide its time so that people would forget about me. Their priority was to avoid negative publicity surrounding my case. By allowing me to go abroad, the Pakistani authorities knew that I would, in all likelihood, receive a substantial amount of media attention.

On May 8, 2019, the Pakistani government issued this official press release: "Asia Bibi has left Pakistan of her own will." It would have been more accurate to write: "After having been detained for seven months against her will in Pakistan, the government permits Asia Bibi to fly to Canada to reunite with her children."

Once I was safely on the plane, the authorities freed Khadim Hussain Rizvi, the leader of the TLP. After I left, there was no revolt in the cities, which proved that the government had succeeded, at least for a time, in muzzling the Islamists.

They may have lost the battle, but I will never feel completely safe. They are tenacious, and so many of them—all around the world—want me dead.

In fact, no sooner had I arrived in Canada than a militant Islamist posted a video online claiming he was in Canada to kill me. In the three-minute-long video, the man claimed to have headed to Alberta. With his face masked, he intoned an Islamic chant, paying homage to the Prophet Muhammad, all while declaring he would massacre "Asia Bibi, the blasphemer." The man added that I would again commit blasphemy but this time abroad and receive a prize for it. "To the enemies of Islam and to the Jewish governments that freed Asia Bibi," he said, "rest assured I am going to kill her!" Canadian authorities took this chilling video very seriously, and so did the European Union, which studied it closely. According to Aman, the results of the investigation concluded that the video was filmed in Pakistan, not in Canada, contrary to what the Islamist claimed. Sounds of street traffic, such as horns from small vans and motorcycles, that are very specific to Pakistan could be heard in the background.

As Ashiq and I were leaving Karachi, the trip seemed endless to us, but our hearts felt lighter. We first landed in Toronto, where we waited a few hours before boarding another plane, and then we got into a car that brought us to our final destination, which I cannot disclose for obvious security reasons. In fact, the Canadian government was very firm on this matter: no pictures and no interviews that might endanger us. As long as I stood on Canadian soil, I was ordered to remain silent on our location. During our journey to Toronto, I signed papers agreeing to this order. Aman, who orchestrated my departure alongside Jan Figel, knew all of the ins-and-outs of the operation. Pakistan agreed to let me go provided that Canada agreed to make me a "mute heroine." Both countries signed the agreement, and I was certainly intent on respecting it because I didn't want to disappoint or endanger my first host country.

And so, after this seemingly endless debacle, we finally reunited with our daughters Eisha and Eisham in a hotel room. I was reclaiming my place with my children and my role as a mother, which imprisonment had deprived me of for so many years. For the first time since that fateful harvest that plunged me into hell, I finally felt free to love, to hope, and to live my life.

Thank you, my God! You lit up the road and showed me the way, that of hope, which delivers and replaces empty dreams with a strong desire to live. I want to cry out with all of my being, thank you, my God!

Chapter 13

LIFE IN A FREE COUNTRY

Make up your minds that happiness depends on being free,
and freedom depends on being courageous.
THUCYDIDES, HISTORY OF THE PELOPONNESIAN WAR

When I reunited with my entire family, I felt like I was experiencing a waking dream. We spent a few days in the hotel looking at each other, smiling, and hugging. Then we moved into a brand-new house in a quiet neighborhood. The long street had about twenty houses of varying sizes lining it, all framed by well-kept gardens. Our house was neither big nor small, but in my eyes, it was a castle compared to our house in Ittan-Walli. The inside was furnished in a modern and comfortable style, and under our feet was a very smooth wood called parquet flooring. I had never seen such a thing. It was quite different from the beaten earth I had always known at home or in my cell. It was anything but unpleasant to walk around barefoot without risking hurting yourself or getting your feet dirty.

Our daughters each had their own room with their own bathrooms, and the kitchen was like the ones seen on advertisements on TV. It, alone, was the size of our old home. It was spacious, overequipped, and flawlessly clean. It was as if no one had ever used it, and it was worthy of a great restaurant or cooking show. I love to cook and felt like a child who had just received ten belated Christmas presents. A representative of the Canadian state showed us around our new home. She was kind to us, and she and her colleague were in charge or of our well-being. One of them would visit us almost every day to help us settle into our new life. Eisham took the bus to school every day, and Eisha, who has several disabilities, finally received care from the best doctors. Her new doctor promised to make Eisha's legs fully straight again so that she can walk normally.

Every month, the Canadian state proved highly generous, helping us pay for the house, food, comfortable clothing, phone bills, and so on. We could not afford a television or a car, but I told Ashiq this was a blessing because we had put on quite a bit of weight from spending seven months cooped up in a miserable room! Every day, we went on long walks to go to the supermarket, which was three kilometers, a little less than two miles, from the house. There was truly nothing better for recovering our health than taking those long walks to do our grocery shopping.

Our first trip to the supermarket left us in shock. The building was huge and filled with enormous products. I don't know if things are similar all over the West, but in Canada, everything is disproportionately large: sandwiches, steaks, bags of fries, shampoo bottles, and even the shopping carts. Everything was radically different from the stalls and corner shops that I had always known at home in the Punjab Province.

As surprising as it may seem, I didn't have too difficult a time adapting to life in the West. My parents were open-minded and let us watch TV from modern countries, and I remembered the kinds of lifestyles I saw on those shows. I knew that people in the West eat using cutlery and that everyone is free to dress however they please without fear of shocking anybody. In fact, I shed my headscarf and wore sneakers and close-fitting clothing without worrying about being judged or getting into trouble. Ashiq also traded in his *shalwar kameez* for fashionable tracksuits, and he couldn't go without them anymore. With his American baseball cap on his head, we would go to the mall every Saturday with the kids and do what they call "shopping" here, and we loved it. We didn't buy much, but it was fun to look.

We felt really good here even though we also felt isolated from not being allowed to talk to anybody, not even the neighbors, in case we were recognized. But we were allowed to use the phone, so I would spend a good part of my day talking with my father, my little sister Nassima, Sidra, whom I had raised as my own daughter, and so on. With smartphones, I could even see my grandchildren, the children of Sidra. I thanked heaven every day and was comforted that I could talk to my family without restrictions, which allowed me to keep a link to my beloved country. I will never be able to thank Canada enough for its hospitality, generosity, and bravery in welcoming someone like me. I will never forget this country! It is where I saw snow for the first time. It was spectacular, magical. The four of us were so happy to fling ourselves into the cold, soft powder.

Our days continued to go by and resemble one another. We were so happy in our safe, little life—far from threat, hatred, and that wretched prison. Then, one ordinary night, we heard a knock on our door. But nobody was supposed to visit us. Whenever our state supervisor friends would visit our home, they always warned us that nobody in the world knew our address. Who on earth could it be? Ashiq, the children, and I froze in fear.

In Urdu, I said, "Who's there?"

No answer.

Then, through the door, a woman's voice called out, "Ashiq?"

The voice sounded kind and shy. Ashiq opened the door but did not scream. In the doorway stood a tall, slender woman with a big smile on her face.

"Surprise!" she said in English.

Ashiq motioned for her to come in and opened his arms for a hug. Stunned, I stared at this woman. She looked like a giraffe and must have been at least two heads taller than me. Even Ashiq seemed small next to her! I figured her intentions must have been good and that Ashiq appreciated her a lot to hug her so tightly. She looked at me and smiled over his shoulder. I had a feeling I had seen her on the BBC before, but I wasn't sure until Ashiq turned to me and said, "This is Anne-Isabelle Tollet, the French journalist who made your story known all around the world and with whom you wrote your first book. She has been helping us since 2010."

I was both astounded and overjoyed to see her standing in my living room. She had found me! Without thinking, I took her in my arms and hugged her very tightly. I understood that she was the first person to be concerned about me and that others took up my cause because of her. It was thanks to this human chain of support that she forged that I made it out of Pakistan alive and free.

While I wasn't familiar with all of the details of her work and support, I knew I owed her a lot. I invited her to sit down on our couch. Sitting next to each other and drinking Pakistani tea, we were both shy but moved. We were meeting for the first time, and while her culture may have been very different from mine, our fates became closely entwined. She told me my hair was wonderful and that I looked like I was in very good shape. I didn't know what to say; I wasn't used to receiving compliments.

We talked a lot through Eisham, who had a good mastery of English. Anne-Isabelle knew so many things about me, my life in prison, and the twists and turns of my experience. I couldn't get over it. Over the course of that lovely evening, we looked at pictures online. She held press conferences all around the world to raise awareness about my fate, and I saw pictures of her in Pakistan in the middle of the Islamists' demonstrations, as well as with my sister Nassima in our home in Ittan-Walli. I told her that she was my soul sister and that if it had not been for her and for God, I would be dead.

The following day, I invited her over for lunch, so I could cook for her. It was my way of expressing my gratitude. I served her Pakistani dishes that I know all the secrets to...with cutlery! I was careful not to make things too spicy because I know that Westerners' digestive systems are very fragile. Despite my caution, she turned beet red with her mouth on fire, and we laughed a lot.

She told me about the idea of writing this book, and I said yes right away. We were such a great team. And for someone who doesn't know how to read, I very much understood how a book can save a life. When Anne-Isabelle had to return to France, we knew we would see each other very soon in Europe. We sent each other pictures and called one another several times a week.

Through my testimony, I would like to be able to help other people in Pakistan who are in the same situation I was in. I suffered for ten years, my children suffered, and it had an enormous impact on my life. I thank the Supreme Court for acquitting me, but so many others need a fair trial too. The world must pay attention to them. To anyone who is suffering in this way, I beg you to remain faithful to your beliefs, even if you are faced with the sword.

If, on that morning of June 14th, the day when everything changed, one of my daughters had had a fever...

If I had not been thirsty...

If I had renounced my Christian faith and converted to Islam...

I would not be here today to encourage you and pray for you.

To those who offered support through prayers, courageous acts, or efforts to spread the news of my story, I don't know words strong enough to express my gratitude. You allowed me to hold my course and not waiver. You gave me strength and hope, and in reading this book, you continue to honor me today.

میرا نام ایشیا ہے اور میں آپ کی زندگی کا مقروض ہوں۔

In my language, that means: My name is Asia, and I owe you my life.

ACKNOWLEDGMENTS

We would like to thank the countless people who worked toward my freedom, particularly Jan Figel for his tireless efforts with the Pakistani authorities.

Muhammad Aman Ullah, who took care of my children and never stopped encouraging me during moments of doubt.

Salman Taseer and Shahbaz Bhatti, who were critical of the blasphemy law and sacrificed their lives in taking up my defense.

I would like to thank my fellow inmate friends and certain members of the prison staff who showed humanity and kindness.

Thank you to the security agencies who kept me alive after I left prison and to the people around the world who prayed for my liberation.

Finally, this book wouldn't have seen the light of day without the crucial support of Isabelle W., Sophie G., Brune, Albéric, Maryam M., and the whole team at the Éditions du Rocher.